BUSINESS
OPPORTUNITIES

Workbook

Vicki Hollett and Michael Duckworth

Oxford University Press

Oxford University Press
Great Clarendon Street, Oxford OX2 6DP

Oxford New York
Athens Auckland Bangkok Bogota Bombay Buenos Aires
Calcutta Cape Town Dar es Salaam Delhi Florence Hong Kong
Istanbul Karachi Kuala Lumpur Madras Madrid Melbourne
Mexico City Nairobi Paris Singapore Taipei Tokyo Toronto Warsaw

and associated companies in
Berlin Ibadan

OXFORD and OXFORD ENGLISH are trade marks of
Oxford University Press

ISBN 0 19 452031 5

© Oxford University Press 1994

First published 1994
Seventh impression 1998

No unauthorized photocopying

Printed in Hong Kong

*The publishers would like to thank the following for their permission to
reproduce photographs:*

Camera Press Ltd: p. 45 (*Dr. Anibal Cavaco Silva*);
Direct Choice: p. 36
The Image Bank: pp. 18 Steve Niedorf, 29 Romilly Lockye,
45 de Moura Machado (*flags*), 60
Innovations: p. 36 (*watch*)
HarperCollins Publishers Ltd: p. 33 Joe Partridge (*Mark McCormack*)
Life File: p. 54-Paul Fisher (*greeting*)
Masayoshi San: p. 24
Network Photographers Ltd: pp. 22 Barry Lewis (*recycling paper*),
Lawrie Sparham (*power station*), 54 Barry Lewis (*Post sauna, Finland*),
Eberhard Grames (*Japanese shoes*)
NHPA: p. 13, BA Janes
Picturepoint Ltd: p. 45 (*Lisbon harbour*)
Raytheon: pp. 14, 15
Retna Pictures Ltd: p. 64
Rex Features Ltd: pp. 22 Peter Brooker (*recycling project*), 25, 48
Stockphotos Inc: p. 45 (*bank*)
Tony Stone Images: pp. 8 Richard Braine, 39, 66 Bruce Ayres.

Illustrations by:

Sophie Grillet: pp. 12, 28, 61, 69
Nigel Paige: pp. 11, 32, 37, 39, 41, 55, 68
Tim Slade: pp. 43, 56
David Williams: p. 42

Photography by:

Rob Judges: pp. 4, 34

Design by:

Mike Brain

Acknowledgements

*The authors and publisher would like to thank the following for
permission to use adapted material and/or to reproduce copyright
material:*

Business Magazines UK Ltd: extracts from articles in *Management
Week*, September 1991
Direct Choice/Innovations (Mail Order) Ltd: extracts from Direct
Choice Christmas Catalogue 1992
The Economist:: extracts and adapted graphs from *The Economist*:,
10.4.93, © *The Economist*, 1993
EMAP Business and Computing Publications: statistics from *Which
Computer*, June 1992
Fortune Magazine; Graham Group PLC: statistics from *The Graham
Bath Report* (Hall Harrison Cowley Public Relations)
HarperCollins Publishers Ltd and the author: cover and adapted
extract from Mark H. McCormack: *Success Secrets* (Fontana)
Martin Manser: extracts from *The Chambers Book of Business
Quotations* edited by Martin H. Manser (published by W. & R.
Chambers Ltd, Edinburgh, 1987)
Raytheon Company: extracts from Annual Report 1992
Softbank Corporation.

Although every effort has been made to trace and contact
copyright holders before publication, this has not always been
possible. If notified, the publisher will be pleased to rectify any
errors or omissions at the earliest opportunity.

Contents

1 Jobs and Responsibilities

1 Making contact

A Here are two conversations where people are meeting one another. Put them in the correct order.

a Good. I've come to take you to your hotel. You'll be staying at the Hilton.
b Just a couple of days. I have to get back as soon as the conference is over.
c Karl Striebel. How do you do? Thank you for coming to meet me.
d Thank you very much. Is it far?
e Fine thanks. How long are you here for?
f It's a pleasure. Did you have a good flight?
g She's the new head of European Sales, isn't she?
h Hello, Josef. How are you?
i No. It only takes about half an hour.
j Hello. I'm Mark Jensen from Ciba Geigy. How do you do?
k That's a shame. By the way, there's someone I'd like you to meet. Caroline Eustace.
l Hi there, Sarah. Nice to see you again.
m Yes, it was fine thanks. No delays.
n That's right. Come on over and I'll introduce you.

Conversation 1		Conversation 2	
Mark	j	Josef	l
Karl		Sarah	
Mark		Josef	
Karl		Sarah	
Mark		Josef	
Karl		Sarah	
Mark		Josef	

B Which conversation is more formal? _____

2 A first meeting

A Peter Berger is a consultant with Prodata, a computer consultancy firm. He is normally based in Geneva but he's working in Bradford at the moment, setting up a new quality control system. On his first day there, he meets Jenny Carlson over lunch.

Put these questions into the correct spaces to complete their conversation.

a *And what exactly are you doing?*
b *What's your job?*
c *Anyway, how long do you think you'll stay in Bradford?*
d *I don't think we've met, have we?*
e *When did you start?*
f *So you're not from Bradford then?*
g *And how long have you worked here?*

Jenny Hello. I'm Jenny Carlson. (1) *I don't think we've met, have we?*

Peter No. Pleased to meet you. I'm Peter Berger from Prodata.

Jenny (2)_____?

Peter No, I'm from Geneva. I'm just working here temporarily.

Jenny Really? (3)_____?

Peter	This morning. Today is my first day.
Jenny	(4)_____?
Peter	I'm setting up a new quality control programme.
Jenny	That's interesting.
Peter	What about you? (5)_____?
Jenny	I work in Sales.
Peter	(6)_____?
Jenny	For eight years. I started as a sales representative and now I'm a regional manager. (7)_____?
Peter	Just three or four months. It depends how long the new system takes to set up.
Jenny	I see. Well, I'm sure you'll enjoy it. It's a very friendly place.

B Now imagine Peter is visiting your company. What will you say when you meet him? Complete this conversation. Invent your own questions and answers this time.

Peter	Hello. I'm Peter Berger from Prodata.
You	_____.
Peter	It's nice to meet you. Do you work here full time?
You	_____?
Peter	I'm just here temporarily.
You	_____?
Peter	Just a couple of weeks. I'm installing a new computer system. What about you? What exactly do you do?
You	_____.
Peter	That's interesting. And how long have you had this job?
You	_____.
Peter	And what did you do before?
You	_____.
Peter	I see. Well, I must dash. I've got a lot to do. It's been nice meeting you.
You	_____.

3 Prepositions

Look at this extract from a company presentation. Fill in the blanks with the words from the box. Use the company organization chart below to help you.

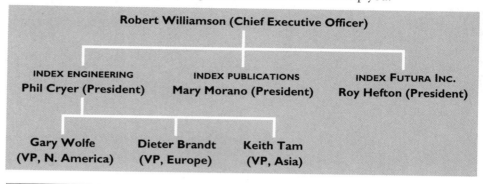

at   for   in   of   of   of   of   of   round   to   to   with

I'd like to tell you a little about some of The Index Group's activities. As you will see from the chart, one of the divisions is Index Engineering. This consists (1) _of_ three groups covering North America, Europe, and Asia. The three Executive Vice Presidents report (2)_____ Phil Cryer, the President and Chief Operating Officer. He, in turn, is accountable (3)_____ Robert Williamson, the Chief Executive Officer. This is my division and I am in charge (4)_____ promotions. I am responsible (5)_____ ensuring that people get to hear about our projects, and I also show clients (6)_____ our headquarters.

The second division is Index Publications, which publishes all kinds (7)_____ scientific magazines as well as a number of different types (8)_____ specialist magazines. There are four major publishing units based (9)_____ New York, Chicago, and Boston.

Now let's look (10)_____ the third division (11)_____ the company. Index Systems recently merged (12)_____ Futura Software development to form this new division, which produces specialist computer software for the engineering industry.

4 Word stress

A   Read these sentences aloud, concentrating on the pronunciation of the words in *italics*.

1   The *products* are manufactured in ten different countries.
    We have *production* facilities in ten different countries.
2   We accept *responsibility* for the damage.
    We are *responsible* for the damage.
3   Craig Sloan has a lot of *expertise* in time management.
    Craig Sloan is an *expert* on time management.
4   I'll explain how we *organize* the project teams.
    I'll explain the *organization* of the project teams.
5   My biggest problem at the moment is how to *motivate* my team.
    My biggest problem at the moment is team *motivation*.

B   Mark which syllable has the main stress in these words.

1   pro|ducts
    pro|duc|tion
2   res|pon|si|bi|li|ty
    res|pon|si|ble
3   ex|per|tise
    ex|pert

4   or|ga|nize
    or|ga|ni|za|tion
5   mo|ti|vate
    mo|ti|va|tion

5 Employment

Complete this puzzle and find the missing word.

1 The bank is planning to _____ over fifty new graduate trainees. (7)
2 As a cost-cutting measure, several senior executives have been _____ redundant. (4)
3 At the age of 65 you will receive an annual _____ equal to two thirds of your final salary. (7)
4 It's easier to get a job if you are in work than if you are _____ . (10)
5 Mr Davis has handed in his _____ and will be leaving at the end of the month. (6)
6 The government should offer generous _____ payments to miners to encourage them to start up their own businesses. (10)
7 You can't _____ her just because she belongs to a trade union. (7)
8 We have to _____ on extra staff in the summer to cope with the extra work. (4)
9 After a boardroom battle, the Chairman was forced to _____ . (6)
10 We hope to avoid compulsory redundancies by encouraging older members of staff to take early _____ . (10)

6 Managing time

A Read this manager's account of her working day. Why is she studying English?

6.45	get up
7.15	drive to work
8.00	start work
6.00	drive home
6.45	cook and eat meal
8.15	household chores
9.15	free time
10.45	go to sleep

I'm Paula Fiocchi and I'm an auditor. I work for a big firm of accountants in Milan. We have an international network of associated firms and I have more and more contact with my counterparts in other countries. I need to be able to discuss Italian accountancy principles with them, so I'm trying to improve my English. It's not always easy to find the time though, as my schedule is pretty hectic.

My job is very interesting but it's very demanding too. I generally start at eight and often don't finish until six at night. The journey to and from work takes about 45 minutes each way and I need to unwind when I get home. I generally have a nice meal with my family. Cooking and eating takes about an hour and a half and I suppose I spend another hour or so on routine chores around the house. It isn't always possible but I like to have an hour and a half of free time if I can. Then it's off to bed. I try to get eight hours' sleep to be sure of being on good form for the next day. It only takes me half an hour or so to get ready in the mornings, because I don't bother with breakfast.

B Calculate how much time Paula has available for her English studies.

C How much time do you have available each day for your English studies?

7 Introducing the team

A An architect is visiting a client's company to discuss a construction project. Read what the project manager says at the start of their meeting.

Good morning. Before we start our meeting, let me introduce you to everyone. I'm Eivind Ebervik, the Vice President with overall responsibility for facilities management within the organization. This is Rosemary Parker, the head of Administrative Services. Mrs Parker directs and co-ordinates all our facilities operations, so she's responsible for space utilization, capital expenditure, maintenance, and security. And the third member of our team is Geoff Dobkin. Mr Dobkin is the Facilities Planning Supervisor, so he is in charge of office-space planning. He's also the leader of the Installations working group.

B Now imagine you are meeting a visitor to your company. Introduce yourself and two other people you work with. Explain what you all do.

1 Good morning. Before we start our meeting, let me introduce you to everyone.

I'm _____

_____

_____

2 This is _____

_____

_____

3 And the third member of our team is _____

_____

_____

2 Telephoning to Make Arrangements

I Changing arrangements

A Read this telephone conversation. Choose the correct words or phrases in *italics*.

Ms Green	Could I speak to Mr Boutin please?
Mr Boutin	Speaking
Ms Green	Hello. *I am/This is* Sarah Green from London. I understand you would like *me to/that I* make a few changes to your itinerary.
Mr Boutin	Yes, that's right. *I prefer/would prefer* to see Ms Watson and Mr Flavell before I meet Mr Trigg. *Would you mind/Would you like* arranging that for me?
Ms Green	*Yes, of course/No, not at all*. I'll set up a meeting with Ms Watson at eleven o'clock and Mr Flavell at twelve.
Mr Boutin	Perfect.
Ms Green	And *do/would* you still like to go to the seafood restaurant for lunch? Perhaps at one instead of twelve?
Mr Boutin	Yes, *I will/that would be nice*.
Ms Green	Good. There's just one other thing though. Mr Trigg won't be able to see you until four o'clock. That doesn't give you much time so would you mind *if I booked/me to book* you on a later flight back?
Mr Boutin	*Yes/No*, that'd be OK.
Ms Green	There's one at 8.15. I'll try to book you a seat.
Mr Boutin	Thanks. I'll leave it to you then. *Would you/ Would you mind* give me a ring later on to confirm everything?
Ms Green	Yes, of course.

B Here is the original itinerary for Thierry Boutin's trip. Look back at the conversation above and make any necessary changes.

```
 9.15   Arrive London Heathrow AF 196. S.Green to
        collect.
11.00   Meeting with Mr Trigg.
12.00   Lunch at Wheeler's Seafood Restaurant with
        S.Green.
 2.00   Meeting with Ms Watson.
 3.00   Meeting with D. Flavell.
 6.30   Return to Paris AF 256. S.Green to take to
        airport.
```

C Write sentences about the visit to explain how the plans have changed.

Example Mr Boutin/meet Jack Trigg/11.00/he/meet him/4.00
Mr Boutin was meeting Jack Trigg at 11.00 but now he's meeting him at 4.00.

1 He/see Ms Watson/2.00/he/see her/11.00

_____

2 Mr Boutin and Mr Flavell/have a meeting/3.00/they/have a meeting/12.00

_____

3 Mr Boutin and Ms Green/go out for lunch/12.00/ they/have lunch/1.00

_____

4 Mr Boutin/return/6.30/he/fly back/8.15

_____

2 Polite questions

A Match each polite question on the left with a sentence from the right that has a similar meaning.

1 Would you mind if I went to the bank?   a   Do you want to go to the bank?
2 Would you mind going to the bank?   b   Go to the bank, please.
3 Would you like me to go to the bank?   c   Please may I go to the bank?
4 Would you like to go to the bank?   d   Do you want me to go to the bank for you?

B Now rewrite these sentences as polite questions. Begin each one with *Would you...*

1 I can send you our latest annual report. Do you want me to?

Would you _____?

2 I'd like a day off next week. Is that OK?

Would you _____?

3 Do you want to fly Business Class?

Would you _____?

4 Please wait a few minutes. The manager is busy at the moment.

Would you _____?

5 Do you want to visit our showroom?

Would you _____?

6 We can pay you in advance if you want.

Would you _____?

7 May I pay by credit card?

Would you _____?

8 Please don't park here. The visitors' car park is over there.

Would you _____?

3 Polite replies

A Read this telephone conversation.

Mr Lopez	Could you put me through to Mrs Clark please?
Receptionist	Who are you?
Mr Lopez	Jorge Lopez.
Receptionist	What?
Mr Lopez	Jorge Lopez.
Receptionist	Wait.
Mr Lopez	Hello. This is Jorge Lopez.
Mrs Clark	What do you want?
Mr Lopez	Could we arrange a meeting to discuss our contract? Are you free this Thursday?
Mrs Clark	No.
Mr Lopez	Oh, that's a pity. How about Friday then, or next Monday?
Mrs Clark	Friday or Monday is OK. I don't care which.

B The two people Mr Lopez talked to were not polite. Write what they should have said.

1 Who are you?

_____

2 What?

_____

3 Wait.

_____

4 What do you want?

_____

5 No.

_____

6 I don't care which.

_____

4 Telephone language

Hidden in this word square are 21 words and expressions to do with telephoning. Can you find them all? (Some are vertical, some horizontal and some diagonal.)

```
P E S W I T C H B O A R D
U E X C H A N G E R Y B I
T H F T G R E C E I V E R
T A P A E M X B R D C L E
H N O H K N M M E I O G C
R G C V O U S G O Q N P T
O U A D N N A I U D N G O
U P L C W G E E O S E J R
G O L I N E D Y N N C M Y
H R T E L O P E R A T O R
B U S Y C H D I A L F A X
```

I'M PUTTING YOUR RUDE CALLER THROUGH NOW.

5 Business expressions

English has a lot of phrasal verbs — verbs that are combined with prepositions to form new verbs with new meanings. Complete the sentences below with phrasal verbs. Choose a word from each column to put in the spaces.

pin	on
is	out
put	off
put	off
pencil	forward
draw	up
look	in
tied	with
bear	up
put	through
come	down

Example Good morning. Could you *put* me *through* to extension 253, please?

1 I've been trying to arrange a meeting with Mrs Tienworn for weeks but she's a difficult woman to _____ _____.

2 I'm afraid I can't make this afternoon's meeting. Something urgent has _____ _____.

3 Shall we _____ _____ next Tuesday? I'll check that I'm free with my secretary and give you a ring to confirm.

4 Tomorrow's meeting _____ _____. Everyone seems to be too busy doing other things.

5 That's settled then. I _____ _____ to seeing you on the 15th.

6 Are you sure it's convenient? I know you're very busy and I don't want to _____ you _____.

7 I think Mr Lee's number has been changed. Could you _____ _____ me a moment and I'll find the new list.

8 We only have a few permanent staff but there are a lot of freelance designers and consultants we can _____ _____ if we need ideas and advice.

9 She asked me to tell you she'll be late. She's _____ _____ in a meeting with a client.

10 There's an emergency at the Manila office. You'll have to _____ _____ your trip to the States and fly out to the Philippines instead.

6 Emergency call

A When an emergency arises, a quick telephone call can prevent a disaster, as this true story shows. Put the different extracts in the right order and find out how a prompt telephone call saved one woman's life.

a   Later that day, the manager phoned the woman and asked her to come back to the store. She told him she couldn't because her car was in the garage for repairs and she lived 25 miles away.

b   But worse was to come. Male tarantulas are usually accompanied by female tarantulas and they hadn't found the female.

c   A woman bought a yucca plant from a well-known British chain store. It died a few weeks later so she took it back to the store and asked for her money back.

d   The store didn't shirk their responsibilities. They replaced the duvet and repaired everything in the house and so this true story had a happy ending — except for the female tarantula, of course.

e   But the manager was very insistent and told her he was sending a taxi out to collect her.

f   The manager told her he couldn't refund her because there are all sorts of reasons why plants die. But he promised to have the yucca analysed and to contact her later.

g   The store sent contract cleaners into the woman's home who took everything apart. They finally found a female tarantula in the duvet on the bed, together with several babies.

h   When she arrived, he took her to his office, gave her tea and biscuits and told her to prepare herself for a shock. The soil of her yucca plant contained a male tarantula.

B Now match each of these words and expressions from the story with the right explanation.

1   a chain store
2   to refund
3   to be insistent
4   soil
5   a tarantula
6   a duvet
7   to shirk responsibilities

a   to demand that someone does something
b   to fail to do what you should
c   a poisonous spider
d   a shop which is part of a group owned by the same company
e   to return a sum of money
f   a bed covering
g   earth, the substance that plants grow in

3 Organizations

1 Present simple and continuous

A Fill in the blanks using the verbs below in the simple present tense.

> be, be, be, have, meet, manufacture, play, provide, own, include

Caloric gas cooker

Raytheon at a glance

Raytheon (1) _____ a diversified, international technology-based company ranked among the 100 largest US industrial corporations. The company (2) _____ four main business segments: Major Appliances, Aircraft Products, Energy & Environmental, and Electronics.

MAJOR APPLIANCES

Our Major Appliances Division (3) _____ an important part in the group's overall sales growth. We (4) _____ the Amana Range of refrigerators, which (5) _____ strict new energy standards, and also produce a wide range of domestic appliances that (6) _____ cookers, freezers and washing machines.

AIRCRAFT PRODUCTS

Our subsidiary, Beech Aircraft, (7) _____ a major player in light jet production, and makes a range of aircraft for business and military use. Beech also (8) _____ nineteen Fixed Base Operations that (9) _____ located in airports nationwide, and that (10) _____ business customers with a complete service including fueling, maintenance and passenger facilities.

Super King Air B200

B Fill in the blanks using the verbs below in the present continuous tense.

> design, grow, become, remove, expand, build, dismantle, reach, work

*Cogeneration plant,
Las Vegas, Nevada*

ENERGY AND ENVIRONMENTAL

Raytheon's Energy and environmental division (1) _____ fast and is a world class competitor in the engineering and construction field.

Under the terms of a new joint venture with Fluor Daniel, our Hydrocarbon Processing Division (2) _____ a $2.2 billion refinery for Raying Refinery company in Thailand.

The Fossil Power division won two large contracts. Currently we (3) _____ a gas-fired power station in Las Vegas and construction work will begin soon. In Colorado, we (4) _____ an existing plant so that it can meet the increased demand for power.

In the field of nuclear power, decommissioning (5) _____ increasingly important, because many nuclear power plants (6) _____ the end of their useful life. We (7) _____ with Long Island Power Authority at the Shoreham Nuclear Generating Station, where we (8) _____ all the systems and we (9) _____ all the contaminated components.

C Fill in the blanks using the verbs below in the simple present or present continuous tense.

> build, carry, combine, detect, develop, have, manufacture, threaten, work, warn

*Terminal Doppler
Weather Radar,
Houston, Texas*

ELECTRONICS DIVISION

Electronics is a key pillar of our strategy for success in the years ahead. In our Missile Division, we (1) _____ advanced missile systems including Patriot, Hawk and Sidewinder. We (2) _____ a multi-billion dollar Patriot Missile contract with the Kingdom of Saudi Arabia and Kuwait. We (3) _____ on the next generation of Patriot and (4) _____ out test firings on the new PAC-3 Multimode missile, which (5) _____ more firepower with improved performance.

We also produce a wide range of radar equipment for military and civilian use. Currently we (6) _____ and testing a new range of transportable Ground-Based Radar systems for the US Army. In the civilian field, the first of 47 Terminal Doppler Weather Radar stations has been built in Texas, and we (7) _____ the next two in Memphis and Atalanta. These weather stations (8) _____ and (9) _____ of severe weather problems that (10) _____ approaching or departing aircraft.

2 Number pronunciation

Choose the correct way of pronouncing the numbers in these sentences.

1 The government have announced a 1.5% reduction in interest rates.
  a 'one point five'
  b 'one comma five'
2 Have you seen the film '2001—A Space Odyssey'?
  a 'twenty oh one'
  b 'two thousand and one'
3 Give me a ring. My number's Oxford 932811.
  a 'nine-three two eight double one'
  b 'ninety-three, twenty-eight, eleven'
4 The reception area in the new building will be 10m x 15m.
  a 'ten metres times fifteen'
  b 'ten metres by fifteen'
5 Fritz Gross joined the company in 1947.
  a 'nineteen hundred and forty-seven'
  b 'nineteen forty-seven'
6 In some countries higher earners pay out 2/3 of their salaries in tax.
  a 'two-thirds'
  b 'two-threes'
7 Our tax year ends on April 30.
  a 'April the thirtieth'
  b 'April thirty'
8 Nicaragua's GNP is approximately $2,000,000,000.
  a 'two million thousand dollars'
  b 'two thousand million dollars'
9 The optimum operating temperature for this equipment is −8°C.
  a 'below eight degrees centigrade'
  b 'minus eight degrees centigrade'
10 The world cup final ended in a 0−0 draw.
  a 'nil−nil'
  b 'zero−zero'

3 Number quiz

A Write the missing figures in these series.

1 eighty-one, nine, sixty-four, eight, _____ , seven
2 love, fifteen, thirty, _____ , game
3 nought point two, nought point two five, nought point three recurring, _____ , one.
4 three, five, seven, eleven, thirteen, _____ , nineteen
5 nineteen eighty-eight, nineteen ninety-two, nineteen ninety-six, two thousand, two thousand and four, _____ ,
6 two hundred and twelve, one hundred, sixty-six, nineteen, _____ , zero

B Which series of numbers relates to

a tennis? __2__
b prime numbers?_____
c leap years?_____
d fractions and decimals?_____
e square roots?_____
f Fahrenheit and Centigrade?_____

4 Business expressions

Complete the sentences using a word from each column.

pick	redundant
get	in my notice
give	a quick word
are	his temper
have	in touch
rushed	her a ring
losing	on call
hand	off our feet
made	and choose

Example   Could I *have a quick word* with you about next week's meeting?

1   The trouble with running your own business is that you _____ 24 hours a day.
2   When the factory closed, 2000 people were _____ .
3   Your doctor phoned while you were out. Could you _____ this afternoon?
4   Sorry I can't spend more time talking with you. We're _____ today.
5   He's not pleasant to work with. He's always _____ and shouting at people.
6   I'll _____ with you later this month and let you know what we've decided.
7   So many people have applied for this position that we can afford to _____ .
8   As soon as I receive your letter confirming that you are offering me the job, I'll go to my boss and _____ .

5 Collecting information

Read this conversation and write the questions A asks.

A   What line of business are you in?

B   Our main activities are construction, real estate, and civil engineering.

A   (1)_____ ?

B   Our headquarters are in Stockholm, Sweden.

A   (2)_____ ?

B   Yes, we have overseas subsidiaries in Germany and in the UK.

A   (3)_____ ?

B   Currently we employ about 8,500 people.

A   (4)_____ ?

B   Our turnover is about $10 million.

A   (5)_____ ?

B   We're doing very well, despite the recession. In fact last year our profits were up.

A   (6)_____ ?

B   No, the real estate market is not doing well at the moment, but we expect that it will improve next year.

A   (7)_____ ?

B   We're building two large bridges in Sweden and a power plant in India.

6 Storing words

A Read these managers' descriptions of how they learn new English words.

'I write the English words I want to remember in lists on my computer, then I can look through them when I have a few free moments at work. I can access them in two ways – via the English word or via the French translation. I also have a program that checks my English spelling and grammar, which is very useful.'
Daniel Marchesin

'I write the words and expressions that I want to learn on individual cards and I keep them in a box file. In the section at the front I keep the new words that I want to learn. I spend a couple of minutes every day looking through them. In the middle are the words that I've half learnt. I try to look at them every week. Then at the back of the box are the words I think I know quite well. I don't look at them very often.'
Anna Balser

'I have a little note book that fits in my pocket. I write words and translations at the back in an alphabetical index. But at the front I store the words in groups under topic headings. They're easier to remember that way – but not so easy to find. That's why I've made an index of topic headings at the front. Whenever I add a new topic, I write it in the index with the page number.'
Koji Nakagawa

B Now look at the three sets of study notes on the opposite page. Only one belongs to one of the managers. Which one?

C Some words are missing from the notes. Complete them with words taken from the box.

Stock	shares	wages
Welfare	get worse	insurance
late	fluctuate	monthly
service	drop	

D Which sets of notes

1 only explain the meaning of words with translations?
2 explain the meaning of words in lots of different ways?
3 show how to pronounce the words?
4 make it easy to find words again when you want them?
5 show how to use words in a sentence?
6 show combinations of words that often appear together in English sentences?
7 could be used to test yourself on the new words?

A

a share (noun) /ʃeə/ — a part of a company sold to investors
'The price of 1 _____ rose today on the 2 _____ Exchange.'

3 _____ industries /sɜː vɪs 'ɪndəstrɪs/ — opposite of manufacturing industries e.g., banking, 4 _____, advertising

to sack someone (verb) — to remove someone from a job

the sack (noun) — 'If he's 5 _____ again, he'll get the sack.'

sharp (adjective) /ʃɑːp/ — 'A sharp rise in prices'
sharply (adverb) — 'Prices rose sharply.'

B

salaire	— salary (paid 6 _____)
	— 7 _____ (paid weekly)
salarié	— wage-earner
sauf avis contraire	— Unless you hear to the contrary
schéma	— diagram, sketch
Sécu	— Social Security (British English)
	— 8 _____ (US English)
sensible	— sensitive
	FALSE FRIEND
	(sensé, raisonnable = sensible)
sérieux	— reliable
société	— company

C

Market Movements

9 _____ □ □□

go up	go down	→ hold firm
increase	fall	remain steady
rise	10 _____	remain stable
raise	decline	
jump	slump	level off
		level out

○ → ◯ grow expand □ □

○ → ○ shrink contract □ □   get better improve □ □   11 _____ deteriorate □ □ □□□

4 Planning Ahead

1 Intentions

A We use *going to* to talk about things that were decided before the moment of speaking. Write what's going to happen in these situations, using the verbs in the box.

not accept   close   correct   resign   repair   retire   update

Example

I've found a mistake in this report.
I'm going to correct it.

1   She doesn't like her job.

_____

2   We don't need this bank account any more.

_____

3   His figures are out of date.

_____

4   This machine is broken.

_____

5   I will be 65 next year.

_____

6   They don't like our offer.

_____

B We use *'ll* (*will*) when we are making a decision at the moment of speaking. Respond to these problems. Make some instant decisions.

A   There's nowhere to park.

B   *Then I'll go by taxi.*

1   A   Her line's engaged.

B   _____

2   A   Your flight's been cancelled.

B   _____

3   A   The lift is full.

B   _____

4   A   He doesn't speak English.

B   _____

5   A   I've lost my pen.

B   _____

6   A   We're about to run out of petrol.

B   _____

2 Future plans

We use *'ll* (*will*) to make instant decisions:

*I've got a headache. I think **I'll take** the day off.*

But we use the present continuous tense to talk about future plans and arrangements:

I can't see him on Monday. I'm taking the day off.

Complete these sentences with *'ll* (*will*) or the present continuous tense.

1   The Holiday Inn have just rung to say they are fully booked. I think I _____ (ring) the Hilton and see if they have any rooms.

2   Could you just remind me what _____ (happen) this afternoon?

3   What time _____ (Mrs Barberis/come) for the meeting and who (give) the presentation?

4   I'm sorry. I have to go now. I _____ (call) you back in about ten minutes.

5   I'm collecting money for a present for Herr Finster. He _____ (retire) next month.

6   I think my credit card must be damaged. Don't worry. I _____ (pay) you cash.

7   I've got to take these anti-malaria pills because I _____ (go) to Africa next month

8   These tickets are Economy Class. Why _____ (we/not/fly) Business Class?

3 Offers, requests, and suggestions

Write what you would say in these situations. Use one of the phrases in the box.

| I'll...   Will you...?   Shall I...?   Could you...?   Would you like me to...? |

1   Your colleague is on her way to see the Sales manager. You know she wants to read a report that you have just finished. What do you say to her?

_____

2   Your boss, who is abroad on business, is on the phone. She urgently wants to see an article about your company that appeared in today's paper. What do you say to her?

_____

3   The Marketing manager is late for a meeting. Perhaps he has forgotten about it and needs reminding. What do you say to the other people at the meeting?

_____

4   An important vistor needs to be shown around the factory this afternoon. You are too busy but you know that your deputy is free. What do you say to him?

_____

5   You have written a highly confidential report. The Director is on the phone and he wants to see it now. What do you say to him?

_____

4 Prepositions

Choose the best word to complete the sentences.

1 He was very nervous before his talk because he was unaccustomed _____ making speeches.

   a to   **b** of   **c** with   **d** on

2 That's an interesting point you are making but I'm not sure it's relevant _____ the discussion.

   a about   **b** to   **c** for   **d** with

3 The Minister said she was confident that there were clear signs _____ an economic recovery.

   a about   **b** in   **c** on   **d** of

4 In hot weather the counter staff may remove their jackets but they mustn't take _____ their ties.

   a away   **b** down   **c** over   **d** off

5 I don't feel qualified to comment _____ the refinancing package because I was not involved in the negotiations.

   a on   **b** at   **c** of   **d** to

6 The Managing Director disagreed _____ the Finance Director about the direction the company should take.

   a with   **b** about   **c** on   **d** over

5 Green issues

Complete this puzzle and find the missing word.

1 We only use _____ paper for our in-house documents. (8)
2 The gases found in some aerosols cause great damage to the _____ layer. (5)
3 The waste from nuclear reactors remains _____ for thousands of years. (11)
4 Many trees in Scandinavia have been killed by _____ rain. (4)
5 Environmentally-_____ products are becoming more and more popular with consumers. (8)
6 Sunlight can be used to make _____ energy, which is completely renewable. (5)
7 The government is trying to persuade motorists to use _____ petrol instead of ordinary petrol in an attempt to reduce pollution. (8)
8 If global _____ continues, sea levels will rise dramatically in the next century. (7)
9 The world's worst _____ accident took place at Chernobyl in 1986. (7)
10 On average, every car produces its own weight of _____ dioxide every year. (6)
11 Unleaded petrol causes slightly less atmospheric _____ than ordinary petrol. (9)

Paper Recycling Plant, London

Fiddler's Ferry Power Station, Liverpool

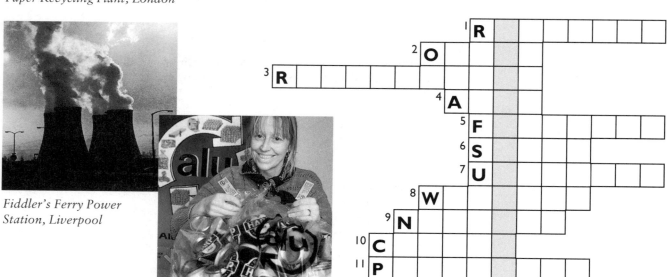

Can Recycling

6 Letter-writing

Study the words and phrases in brackets and choose the correct words or phrases.

Dear [1](Sir/Mr Jacobs/Mr Sales Manager),

With [2](relation/reference/connection) to our telephone [3](dialogue/meeting/conversation) today, I am [4](posting/enclosing/including) our latest catalogue. I [5](am afraid/deeply regret/apologize) that our most up-to-date price list is not yet available, but I shall send you one as soon as they are printed.

May I draw your attention to the products listed on pages 20 and 21, which are specifically designed for frozen foods and which meet the most recent environmental regulations? If you [6](wish/need/like), we would be happy to supply you with any samples you may require.

If you have any further [7](questions/enquiries/doubts), or would like to arrange a meeting, please do not [8](pause/delay/hesitate) to [9](connect/contact/correspond) us again.
In the meantime, I [10](look/wait/expect) forward to [11](listening/hearing/seeing) from you.

[12](Rgds.,/Yours sincerely,/Love from),

J. P. Poulson

J P Poulson
Sales Manager

[13](Enc./tnks/p.p.)

Dear Mr Poulson,

[14](Thanks/Thank you/I am grateful) for your letter of August 18.

I am [15](pleased/happy/overjoyed) to tell you that we are interested in ordering your environmentally-friendly packaging materials for our new range of frozen foods.

I [16](shall/will/would) be grateful [17](when/if/that) you [18](may/could/should) come and see us on Monday 11th September at 10.00 a.m. to discuss our requirements in detail. If this date is not [19](correct/available/convenient), I would [20](like/appreciate/want) it [21](when/so/if) you could give me a ring on 01889 334573, extension 285.

Please find [22](inside/within/enclosed) a map of how to get to our factory, which is on the Westway Industrial estate.

I look [23](forward/towards/ahead) to meeting you on September 11th.

Yours [24](faithfully/sincerely/for ever),

P D Jacobs

P D Jacobs
Managing Director

5 Growth and Development

1 A career history

Masayoshi San is the founder of SOFTBANK, Japan's leading software distribution company. Complete his account of his career history using time expressions from the box.

Before when at soon from Since later to until In after

I was born in 1957 in a small town on Kyushu Island in Japan. My family stayed there (1) _____ I was nearly 13, then we moved to Hakata so that I could go to a better school. My family were very poor and (2) _____ that time, Korean people were discriminated against, so I used to try and hide the fact that I was Korean.

But that all changed three years (3) _____ when I went to the States to go to High School and University. I stayed there (4) _____ 1973 (5) _____ 1979 and my experiences in the US affected my whole way of thinking about life. (6) _____ going there, I had been nervous about being Korean and using my Korean name but now I use it all the time.

I started SOFTBANK two years (7) _____ I returned to Japan and my first break came (8) _____ I got a contract to buy software for Joshin Denki. (9) _____ those days they were the biggest store specializing in PCs in Japan. As (10) _____ as people knew I was supplying Joshin Denki, they all started doing business with me and my monthly revenues went up from $10,000 to $2.3m in one year. (11) _____ then, our sales revenues have gone up every year, and now we distribute 50% of the software sold in Japan.

2 A company history

Read through the notes about Eagleair, then ask and answer questions about the company using the prompts.

1984	Edwin North sets up Eagleair, producing light aircraft for the leisure market from a factory in Wales
1987	George Corby, a talented helicopter designer, joins Eagleair.
1988	Eagleair produce their first light helicopters using engines imported from the USA.
1990	Eagleair stop producing light aircraft and concentrate on helicopters.
1990	Eagleair move to a new factory in Dorset and start making their own engines. George Corby is appointed Vice Chairman.
1991	Eagleair win a contract to supply helicopters to the Zimbabwe police.

Examples

How long / Mr North / run Eagleair?
How long has Mr North been running Eagleair?
He's been running Eagleair since 1984

How long / they / be based in Wales?
How long were they based in Wales?
They were based in Wales for six years.

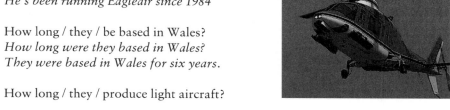

1   How long / they / produce light aircraft?

_____

2   How long / George Corby / work for Eagleair?

_____

3   How long / they / manufacture helicopters?

_____

4   How long / they / use engines imported from the US?

_____

5   How long / they / have a factory in Dorset?

_____

6   How long / George Corby / be Vice-Chairman?

_____

7   How long / they / supply helicopters to the Zimbabwe police?

_____

_____

3 Social conversations

Read these conversations and complete the replies in an appropriate way. Use the words in brackets and the present perfect simple or continuous tense.

A I bumped into Roger yesterday. Did you know he was made redundant? (be unemployed)

B Yes, it's very sad — *he's been unemployed for months.*

A I hear the receivers have been called in at Pelican Pools. (lose money)

B I'm not surprised — *they have been losing money for years.*

1 **A** I didn't know you were keen on golf. (play golf)

   B Didn't you? _____

2 **A** You two have met before, haven't you? (know each other)

   B That's right. _____

3 **A** What's wrong. I'm not late, am I? (wait)

   B I'm afraid you are. _____

4 **A** What's that funny noise? Is it my car alarm? (ring)

   B Yes, it is. _____

5 **A** What a lovely car! Is it new? (have)

   B No, it isn't actually. _____

6 **A** Is his number still engaged? (talk to someone)

   B Yes, it is. _____

7 **A** So what makes you think you deserve a pay rise? (do the manager's job)

   B It's simple. _____

4 Word partnerships

Eight verbs are missing from these lists. What are they? Put the verbs in the correct tense and fill in the spaces. Be careful—they are all irregular.

Infinitive	Simple past	Past participle
spend money	*spent* time	*spent* more than you earn
1 _____ your temper	_____ money	_____ your job
2 _____ a profit	_____ a decision	_____ mistakes
3 _____ a company	_____ a risk	_____ into trouble
4 _____ care	_____ a message	_____ a holiday
5 _____ someone out	_____ shares	_____ a new car
6 _____ on strike	_____ on holiday	_____ bankrupt
7 _____ a presentation	_____ in your notice	_____ someone a present
8 _____ the newspaper	_____ a report	_____ through your notes

5 Saying what happened

A Match each phrase in column A with three appropriate phrases from column B. The sentences end in three different ways — with the past simple, the past continuous, or the past perfect tense.

Example

They invited me for an interview...   and they offered me the job.
while I was working for another bank.
after they had read my CV.

A
1   The board awarded all the staff a 10% pay rise...
2   Mr Cavalli read the report...
3   We managed to find an agent in Ankara...
4   She was sent on a training course...

B
a   while he was waiting for his plane.
b   while she was working in the publicity department.
c   that his deputy had written.
d   and she was later promoted to assistant manager.
e   after we had advertised in the Turkish trade press.
f   because the company had done very well that year.
g   and wrote his comments in the margin.
h   and started exporting our fabrics there within a week.
i   because she had had so little experience of copy writing.
j   because the rate of inflation was increasing.
k   while we were attending a trade fair there.
l   so the unions decided not to go on strike.

B   Now think of three different ways of completing these sentences. Try to use three different past tenses in your answers.

1   I decided to apply for a new job...

a _____

b _____

c _____

2   My company sent me on an English course...

a _____

b _____

c _____

3   I thought of a way of solving the problem...

a _____

b _____

c _____

6 Business expressions

Complete the sentences below. Choose a word or phrase from each column to put in the spaces.

press   venture
with   papers
expense   share
glass   or return
start   accounts
working   world
sale   from scratch
market   cuttings
third   reference to
joint   ceiling

Example   There's no risk to you if you stock our products. Our terms are *sale* or *return*.

1   In the nineteen-eighties, many banks made large loans to _____ _____ nations, which later had to be written off.

2   We'd like to set up a _____ _____ with a German company so we can draw on their marketing expertise and share the risks.

3   The senior managers all have _____ _____ that they use to entertain clients.

4   I am writing _____ _____ your letter of 11th May.

5   I'll show you the file of _____ _____ and you can see what the papers have been saying about the company.

6   Many women feel there is a _____ _____ that prevents them from gaining seats on the boards of their companies.

7   The computer virus destroyed all the work we'd done so we had to _____ _____.

8   We were forced to reduce our prices in order to maintain our _____ _____.

9   We send all the participants the _____ _____ a week before the conference starts. Then they have plenty of time to read them.

6 Problem Solving

1 A meeting

Read this extract from a meeting. Choose the correct words or phrases in italics.

Elena The next item on the agenda is Kilman & Co. Could you bring us up to date on this problem, Claus?

Claus Yes, they're slow payers. They know our terms are 30 days but they're always two or three months late. They now owe us £85,000 and it's three months past the due date. I think we *ought/should/would* take them to court.

Reza No, that's simply not *manageable/feasible/permissible*. They always pay us eventually and we need their business. They're talking about placing another large order with us next month.

Elena So what do you think we should *do/doing/to do*?

Reza *Why/Which/How* about *negotiate/negotiating/to negotiate* a longer credit period with them next time? We *could/better/shall* adjust our prices accordingly.

Elena That *perhaps/might/will* be the answer for future deals.

Claus I *think/not think/don't think* we should accept any more orders from them. They'll break the terms of the contract. If George Stephens *is/was/would be* still there, everything *will be/would be/is* fine. But they've got a new Finance Director and that's the problem. He just ignores all my letters. I really think we *would/did/had* better *start/to start/starting* taking legal action to show that we're serious.

Elena I'm not sure *on/about/with* that. At least not yet. Why *aren't/don't/won't* we set up a meeting with the new Finance Director? If we *will get/get/got* to know him personally, he *will be/was/is* much easier to deal with.

Reza *Here's/You have/That's* a good idea. Shall I arrange something? We *could/better/need* all go out to the Manor.

Claus All right, but if it *wouldn't/won't/doesn't* work, we *will/would/better* have to get the lawyers in.

2 Making suggestions

A Match each comment in column A with the correct reply from column B.

A

1 Their office doesn't seem to be on the map.
2 Is this spray gun worth repairing?
3 Where shall we hold the office party?
4 My interview's at nine—in London.
5 They've asked for a 50% discount.
6 How can we improve the brochure?
7 She's got to see these designs today.
8 Lunch?

B

a That's simply not feasible and they know it.
b That's a good idea.
c We could make the cover more attractive.
d I think we should just buy another one.
e You'd better ask them for directions.
f You'd better not be late.
g How about hiring a houseboat on the river?
h Why don't you fax them then?

B Now think of three different suggestions to make in these situations. Use the phrases in the box.

> I think we should...   How about...?   We could...
> We'd better...   Why don't we...?

Example

You are in the soft drinks business. One of your competitors is running an aggressive advertising campaign and taking some of your market share. What do you suggest to your marketing team?

I think we should change our advertising agency.

We'd better cut our prices.

Why don't we run a new promotional campaign targeted at children?

1 You are talking to your Finance Director. You need to reduce the day-to-day running costs of your office or some staff will have to be made redundant. What do you suggest?

_____

_____

2 You and your colleague are travelling to an important meeting next Monday. You have just heard that there will be a public transport strike that day.

_____

_____

3 You are discussing a problem with your personnel manager. Your best supervisor has taken three days off and been late five times in the last month. She has worked for the company for over twenty years and she is usually very reliable.

_____

_____

3 Pronunciation

These words are all written in phonetic symbols. Work out what the words are, using the phonetic alphabet in your dictionary if necessary, then write them out in normal English script.

1 /ˈbɪznɪs/   _business_
2 /gærənˈtiː/   _____
3 /ɪnˈʃɔːrəns/   _____
4 /əˈdʒendə/   _____
5 /ˈwɒrentiː/   _____
6 /nɪgəʊʃɪˈeɪʃn/   _____
7 /ˈkɒliːg/   _____
8 /ədˈvaɪs/   _____
9 /ˈkwɒntətɪ/   _____
10 /ˈdɪskaʊnt/   _____

4 Future possibilities

Put the verbs into the correct tense. Use *will* and the present tense if you think the person is talking about something which might happen. Use *would* and the past tense if they are talking about something which is unlikely or impossible.

Example

I've got his number — if there *are* (be) any problems, I *will let* (let) him know.

I *would phone* (phone) him if I *had* (have) his number but I don't know what it is.

1 If I _____ (have) time, I _____ (read) your report and I'll let you have my comments by Monday.

2 I _____ (pick) you up at the airport myself if I _____ (not/have) any appointments on Tuesday, and then we can go for a meal together.

3 If she _____ (have) a little more experience, she _____ (be) perfect for the job, but as it is, I don't think she's the right person.

4 The whole division has been performing badly ever since he was appointed Managing Director. Things _____ (be) very different if I _____ (be) still in charge.

5 I've got your number so if Jack _____ (ring) from New York this afternoon, I _____ (pass) it on to him.

6 I've decided not to take the job because I _____ (hardly/see) my children at all if I _____ (have to) travel so much.

7 I _____ (show) her your designs if I _____ (see) her this afternoon, and then I can tell you what she thinks of them tomorrow.

8 The Financial Manager is coming to the meeting with me and if there _____ (not/be) any last minute hitches, we _____ (sign) the contract this afternoon.

9 It's a pity Mrs Falworth is away. If she _____ (be) here, I'm sure she _____ (be) able to give you an answer.

10 Unfortunately my father has a fixed pension. If it _____ (be) index-linked, it _____ (go) up with inflation.

5 Negotiations quiz   Look at the quiz below. Decide which of these answers you agree with most and check your score to find out.

WHAT SORT OF A NEGOTIATOR ARE YOU?

1 **In a negotiation, do you:**
- A like to show you are trying to understand the other side's point of view?
- B show little or no sympathy for the other side's point of view?

2 **You know the other side is very keen to make a deal with you. Do you:**
- A show you are willing to compromise so you can reach an agreement?
- B point out that it's important for them to get your agreement?

3 **When you are telling the other side about your objectives, do you:**
- A speak openly and honestly?
- B lie in order to get more concessions?

4 **The other side has made an error. If you point it out, you can make them look foolish. Do you:**
- A ignore it?
- B draw attention to it?

5 **Things aren't going your way. The other side isn't making enough compromises. Do you:**
- A try approaching the problem from a different angle?
- B threaten to walk out if you don't get more concessions?

6 **Do you want the other side in a negotiation to leave feeling:**
- A satisfied?
- B dissatisfied?

More As than Bs
You see negotiations as problem solving exercises. You try to understand the position of your negotiating partners and establish an atmosphere of trust and mutual co-operation. Your negotiating style is probably best suited to situations where your broad goals are different to the goals of the other side, for example negotiations between customers and suppliers.

More Bs than As
You see negotiations as conflict situations. There's only one pie as far as you're concerned, and you are not prepared to let anyone take your share. Your negotiating style is probably best suited to situations where your broad goals are similar to the goals of the other side, for example negotiations between management and unions.

6 Clinching a deal

What are the secrets of successful selling? Read this story from *Success Secrets* by Mark McCormack, the American management guru, and find out how one of his sales executives managed to strike a deal.

Complete the passage with phrasal verbs from the box. Be careful—some verbs need to be changed into the past tense.

> point out   come up with   stay up   run out of   look through
> slip out   turn out   get round to   find out

One of our sales executives had to give an important sales presentation. He (1)_____ late so that he could (2)_____ his notes and get prepared. The next morning, he flew several thousand miles to the company headquarters and got ready.

From the start, nothing went right. The photocopier (3)_____ paper so he had to get copies made in another office; the conference video machine wasn't working, and the clients all arrived late. When he finally (4)_____ giving his talk, several people (5)_____ of the room saying they had other appointments. Worse still, there was no way he could (6)_____ who was in charge.

Our executive decided to (7)_____ that this kind of reception was not what he had expected. 'This isn't right,' he said, 'I've travelled four hours to see you. I won't waste my time and yours.'

'You're not wasting your time,' said a young woman who (8)_____ to be the associate director of marketing, 'I make the decisions here.'

This was precious information. Armed with this knowledge, he (9)_____ the idea of a smaller meeting and he managed to make a sale.

7 Telephoning to Exchange Information

1 Asking questions

A Read this account of a telephone call. Write the questions the customer asked.

Autorecambios Torrejón are on the phone. They want to know if we have dispatched their order yet.

Have you dispatched our order yet?

Example

1 And they want to know when we dispatched it.

_____

2 They'd like to know how many different shipments there are.

_____

3 And they want to know whether the first shipment contains the Rapidex plugs.

_____

4 They want to know when it will arrive.

_____

5 And they'd like to know if we've received their payment for their last order.

_____

6 And they also want to know if we are giving them a 10% discount.

_____

B Now look at some more questions. They are all direct questions. Change them into indirect questions and put them in the correct places in the conversation.

Are there any seats available?
When do they want to leave?
What are the options?
Would they mind flying with Singapore Airlines?
When will the tickets arrive?
How long are they staying?
Are there any British Airways flights around that time?

Annie Bradley's Travel. Anne Bradley speaking.
José Hello Anne. This is José Cabinda. I need a couple of flights to Bangkok for our sales managers. Can you tell me (1) *what the options are?*
Annie Certainly. Could you tell me (2)_____
José Friday June 18th.
Annie And do you know (3)_____
José Yes, five days. They'd like to come back on the 24th. Could you tell me (4)_____
Annie I'll have a look. No, nothing with BA I'm afraid. Do you think (5)_____
José No, I'm sure they wouldn't.
Annie Good. There's a flight on the 18th at 8.30. It gets in the same day at 9.30 in the evening.
José Do you know (6)_____
Annie Yes, there are. I've just called it up on the screen. Shall I book you two now?
José Yes, please. And that's Club class, OK? Do you know (7)_____
Annie In four or five days. I'll send them to you as soon as they come in.

2 Checking and correcting

Complete this telephone conversation. Choose the correct words or phrases in italics.

Una   Hans, I've got the details about the break in. I think we'd better get a letter off to the insurance company today.

Hans   OK, *wait/stay/hang* on a second — I'll just get the file.

Una   *Ready?/Steady?/Set?*

Hans   Yes, *begin/fire/speak* away.

Una   Now, the date of the break-in was the thirteenth.

Hans   Sorry, *was that/I repeat/did you speak* the thirtieth?

Una   No, the thirteenth. And you've got the list of what was stolen, haven't you?

Hans   Yes — the two Macs, the scanner and the laser printer. Is that *a lot/everything/finished*?

Una   No, *I say/there's/it is* one more thing. They took the portable phone as well.

Hans   Ah yes.

Una   It all comes to £6,961.

Hans   Uh huh. And can you *tell/say/speak* me the policy number?

Una   Yes, it's KHT 33982775. I've got all the original invoices if they query anything.

Hans   Right, I'll send off the claim today. Could we just *repeat/see/run* over that again?

Una   *Probably/Definitely/Certainly*.

Hans   The break-in was on the thirteenth and we're claiming £6,961 for the Macs, the scanner, the laser printer and the phone. And the policy number is KHT 33982775. *Are they/Is that/Have I* it?

Una   Yes, that's *that/the lot/it all*.

3 Explanations

Complete the spaces in these sentences. Use *who/that*, *which/that*, *when/that*, *where* or *whose*.

Example

Monday 19 October 1987 was Black Monday, the day *when* stock markets all over the world crashed.

1   I'm looking for a place _____ we can hold next year's sales conference.

2   Is there anybody here _____ can give me some advice about trains to Paris?

3   He wants to come and see us in week 36, but that's the week _____ we move to the new offices.

4   Rob Davies. I seem to remember that name. Isn't he the man _____ cheque bounced?

5   We're prepared to reduce the price of the goods _____ are approaching their sell-by date.

6   You know that restaurant in Seoul _____ there's a big white grand piano? It's burnt down.

7   We take on extra staff at Christmas. That's the time of year _____ we are at our busiest.

8   I'm calling about the advertisement _____ appeared in today's *Times*.

9   I'd like to introduce you to Lucyna Swolkien. Lucyna is the lady _____ discovered the formula.

10   I'm looking for the person _____ car is in my parking space.

4 Product descriptions

A Look at the products in the *Direct Choice* executive gift catalogue. Is there anything you would like to buy?

DESKMATE

Desktop shredder for only £19.95

Desktop Shredder
CH830 £19.95
Mains Adaptor
CH831 £9.95

NIGHTVISIONS

Night Vision Glasses
CS022 £9.95
Night Vision Clip On
CS029 £9.95

JUNGHANS

Junghans Solar Watch (ladies)
CR196 £99.95
Junghans Solar Watch (mens)
CR197 £89.95

SARACEN

Protect yourself and your family wherever you go
Saracen Alarm Code **£89.95**

MER

Restore that showroom shine

Mer Polish
500ml
CD418 £9.95
1000ml
CD419 £14.95
3000ml
CD420 £29.95

PENTECH 2000

Free Ball-Point and Fine Liner with Pentech 2000

Pentech 2000 + set
CH855 £19.95
Two sets
CH861 £37.50
Three sets
CH862 £50.00

IMATRONIC

Perfect presentations with a laser pointer

Laser pen pointer
CH854 £95.00

B Match each product in column A with the correct description from column B and the special features from column C.

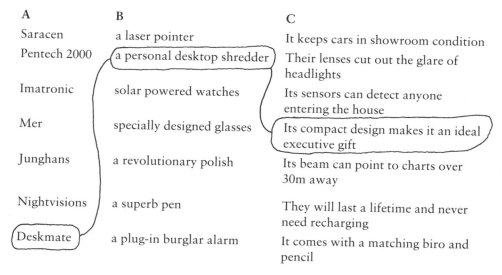

A	B	C
Saracen	a laser pointer	It keeps cars in showroom condition
Pentech 2000	a personal desktop shredder	Their lenses cut out the glare of headlights
Imatronic	solar powered watches	Its sensors can detect anyone entering the house
Mer	specially designed glasses	Its compact design makes it an ideal executive gift
Junghans	a revolutionary polish	Its beam can point to charts over 30m away
Nightvisions	a superb pen	They will last a lifetime and never need recharging
Deskmate	a plug-in burglar alarm	It comes with a matching biro and pencil

C Now use the information to write product descriptions.

Example   *Deskmate is a personal desktop shredder whose compact design makes it an ideal executive gift.*

D Write a catalogue description for a brand new product that you have invented. Draw a sketch, explain what the product does, and include information on any special features.

5 Payments

Complete this puzzle and find the missing word.

1   We _____ the bill but were told it was correct. (7)
2   If you have got the receipt, the shop will _____ your money or exchange the goods. (6)
3   I am writing to_____ the order for 1800 Rapidex plugs which we discussed this morning. (7)
4   If you_____ the cheque, they won't be able to cash it for another ten days. (8)
5   We'd like to_____ an order for 18 Panasonic NVB6 camcorders. How many do you have in stock? (5)
6   I'm sorry about the delay. I'll _____ a cheque in the post to you today. (3)
7   We should ask both companies to _____ us a quotation before we decide which one to use. (4)
8   There was no money in his account so the cheque _____ . (7)
9   If you have paid the invoice in the last few days, please _____ this reminder. (6)

6 Business expressions

Complete the sentences with a verb from column A and a word or phrase from column B.

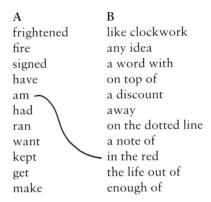

A	B
frightened	like clockwork
fire	any idea
signed	a word with
have	on top of
am	a discount
had	away
ran	on the dotted line
want	a note of
kept	in the red
get	the life out of
make	enough of

Example   They have paid my salary cheque into the wrong bank account and as a result I *am in the red.*

1 We're going to place a large order with them so see if you can _____ _____.
2 We've been very busy but everything is under control and we have _____ _____ the work.
3 Yes, I'm ready now. I've got my pen and paper so _____ _____.
4 Could I _____ _____ those figures you mentioned so I don't forget them?
5 Do you _____ _____ when Elena will be back? I need to see her rather urgently.
6 There were no problems with the deliveries. The whole operation _____ _____.
7 I've _____ _____ my boss. He does nothing but criticize. I'm going to apply for a transfer.
8 The contract negotiations lasted nine hours, but in the end everyone _____ _____.
9 The road was wet, my brakes failed and the car skidded across the road. It _____ _____ me.
10 Do you have a moment? I _____ _____ you about your sales targets.

8 Visitors

1 Meeting friends

While on a visit to his company's London office, Koji Yaegashi called in on his old friend Jack Walker. Put their conversation in the correct order.

1 Jack It's good to see you again. How are you?
2 Koji I'd love to, but I'm seeing some clients this evening. What about tomorrow?
3 Jack Great. We'll see you tomorrow then.
4 Koji Just a couple of days then I'm back off to Tokyo.
5 Jack Oh, we're fine. How long are you staying?
6 Koji What time shall I come?
7 Jack Hello Koji. What are you doing here? *1*
8 Koji No, it's all right. I've got a hire car.
9 Jack What a pity it's not for a bit longer. Anyway, how about dinner tonight?
10 Koji Oh, fine thanks. And you and Jane?
11 Jack That'd be lovely. Jane will be pleased.
12 Koji Hi. I've got a few people to see upstairs so I thought I'd drop in and say hello. *2*
13 Jack How does eight to eight thirty suit you? Do you need a lift?

2 Polite replies

Match each comment with a suitable reply.

1 We've just won that large contract with ICI.
2 Here, let me pay.
3 Our sales manager is in hospital.
4 It's not good news. They say they might have to make me redundant.
5 I'm just off to my interview.
6 I'm so sorry we're late.
7 Do have a seat.
8 Would you mind waiting for a moment?
9 Thank you very much.
10 It's been a lovely party but I'm afraid I must be going.

a Good luck.
b It's a pleasure.
c No, please, I insist. The drinks are on me.
d What a pity! Lovely to see you anyway.
e Congratulations!
f No, not at all.
g I am sorry. Bad luck!
h That's all right. We haven't started yet.
i Thank you.
j Oh dear! Nothing serious I hope.

3 Requests and offers

Choose the best word to complete the sentences.

1 _____ you possibly give me a lift to the airport tomorrow?
   a Will   b Could   c Would   d May

2 It's a bit hot in here. Would you mind if _____ the window a bit?
   a I opened   b open   c you open   d you opened

3 Here's that letter for Mrs Al-Rabi. _____ you make sure it catches this afternoon's post?
   a May   b Will   c Shall   d Do

4 Excuse me. _____ a beer please?
   a Give me   b I want   c Would I have   d Could I have

5 My name's Mrs Caporossi. _____ tell Mr Ellingham that I'm here?
   a May you   b Would you mind c Could you   d Do

6 I _____ the line's busy at the moment. Will you hold?
   a fear   b apologize   c feel sorry   d am afraid

7 I seem to have lost my pen. _____ borrow yours?
   a Will I   b Would you   c Can I   d Shall you

8 Waiter. _____ we have the bill please?
   a Will   b Shall   c Would   d Could

9 I'm a bit tied up at the moment. Would you mind _____ me back later this afternoon?
   a call   b calling   c to call   d called

10 Good afternoon Mrs Czuba. _____ you like to take a seat while I tell Mr Chaillot you're here?
   a Will   b Would   c Could   d May

4 Experiences

Complete this conversation. Put the verbs in brackets into either the present perfect or the simple past tense.

A Do you travel much in your job?

B Yes, quite a lot.

A (1)_____ (you/ever/be) to the Far East?

B Yes, I go there quite regularly. In fact I (2)_____ (go) to Thailand a couple of weeks ago. Do you know that part of the world?

A Yes, I do. I (3)_____ (live) in Bangkok for three years when I was a child; my father (4)_____ (be) in the Diplomatic Service but he's retired now.

B Really? (5)_____ (you/ever/be) back there?

A Yes. I (6)_____ (take) my family there for a holiday last year.

B (7)_____ (you/have) a good time?

A Oh yes. We (8)_____ (enjoy) it a lot.

B As a matter of interest, where (9)_____ (you/stay)?

A We (10)_____ (stay) at the Oriental Hotel in Bangkok, and then we (11)_____ (travel) down to Ko Samui and (12)_____ (have) a holiday on the beach.

B What a coincidence — I (13)_____ (stay) at the Oriental too the other week. I can understand why they say it's the best hotel in the world. It's certainly the most wonderful hotel I (14)_____ (ever/stay) in.

5 Social quiz

Do you know what to say on social occasions? Choose the best word or phrase for these situations.

1   What would you say to someone on their 27th birthday?
   a   Congratulations.   b   Happy birthday.
   c   Joyous birthday.   d   Happy anniversary.

2   The taxi fare is £8.30 so you give the taxi driver £10. What do you say?
   a   The tip is yours.   b   The change is yours.
   c   Keep the tip.   d   Keep the change.

3   You didn't hear what someone said. What do you say?
   a   I apologize.   b   Please repeat.
   c   I didn't hear.   d   Sorry?

4   You want to attract a waiter's attention in a restaurant. What do you say?
   a   Waiter!   b   Sir!
   c   Over here!   d   Come, please!

5   Your colleague tells you he can't come to your party. What do you say?
   a   How shameful.   b   I don't care.
   c   What a pity.   d   You don't matter.

6   Your English client says, 'I'll get the first round'. Where are you?
   a   At a boxing match.   b   On a golf course.
   c   In a pub.   d   In a car.

7   The person you are playing golf with has just missed a shot. What do you say?
   a   Good luck.   b   Bad luck.
   c   Bad chance.   d   Sorry.

8   The person you are playing golf with has just made a good shot. What do you say?
   a   Good shot!   b   Good chance!
   c   Well shot!   d   Good luck!

9   The hostess says, 'Thank you for the flowers, they're beautiful.' What do you say?
   a   Don't mention them.   b   It's a pleasure.
   c   They're OK.   d   Please.

10 You meet an old friend at a conference. She says, 'Lovely to see you. How are things?' What do you say?
   a   How do you do?   b   Very well, thank you.
   c   Fine, thanks.   d   Good.

6 Expressions

Complete the sentences using a word from each column.

for	sending
of	moving
without	saying
at	buying
about	being
on	having
for	going
of	keeping
to	hitting
in	sorting

1 I enjoy golf but I'm not very good *at hitting* the long shots.
2 Would you be interested _____ a look at the new factory?
3 I must apologize _____ you waiting.
4 I'm just calling to thank you _____ the problem out so quickly.
5 I expect you're looking forward _____ away on holiday next week.
6 Why don't you ring them up instead _____ them a fax?
7 I'm surprised that he left _____ good-bye.
8 You can try asking them for credit but they'll probably insist _____ paid in advance.
9 She's unhappy _____ to a new town.
10 I'm thinking _____ a new camera. Do you know anything about them?

7 Food

How good is your restaurant menu vocabulary? Look at this word square and find the names of: six vegetables, five fruits, four herbs and spices, three kinds of fish, two kinds of shellfish, four meats, and two kinds of poultry.

8 Conversation topics

Read these short extracts from different conversations. In each one someone is telling a visitor about their country. Which ones are talking about

1   a festival?
2   the climate?
3   natural resources?
4   the TV network?
5   politics?
6   the economy?
7   the tax laws?
8   a local drink?
9   a national sport?
10   the currency?

a   There are a hundred öre to the krone and each krone is worth around 10p.
b   Our biggest problem is the balance of payments. There's a huge deficit.
c   In the spring, when the cherry blossoms are out, hundreds of people gather under the trees for picnics.
d   You have to be careful it doesn't burn your throat. Some people put it in the deep freeze for a while, so it's icy cold when they swallow it.
e   Everyone has a personal allowance, then the rate you pay depends on how much you earn.
f   We've just changed from a proportional representation system to a first past the post system. So instead of working out the total votes cast for each party, we count up the votes in each constituency and the winner is elected.
g   You have to wrap up really warm. Minus 10 or 15 degrees is quite common, so you need a hat that covers your ears.
h   We have six channels. Two are state run and four are commercial but we can pick up quite a few foreign stations too.
i   You have a wooden puck and you have to try and hit it into the other team's goal.
j   There are the mountains of course. They provide us with hydroelectric power, and we have a few copper and tin mines, but that's all in the way of minerals.

43

9 Reporting on Progress

1 Preparations

A Complete this conversation. Put the verbs in brackets into the present perfect tense.

Paola How are you getting on with the arrangements for the trade fair?

Luis Quite well. I *'ve rung* (ring) the organizers and _____ (reserve) the stand. I _____ (tell) them we need five metres. Is that OK?

Paola Yes, that's fine. _____ (you/hire) the display equipment yet?

Luis No, I _____ (not/finalize) that yet. I thought I'd check that five metre figure with you first. But I _____ (speak) to the suppliers and there won't be any problems getting hold of it.

Paola Good. How is the publicity coming on?

Luis OK. One of the sales managers _____ (already/do) a mail shot to local customers, but I _____ (not/write) the copy for the brochure of exhibitors yet. I'll do it tomorrow and let you have a look at it.

Paola Yes, you'd better get a move on with that. I _____ (draw up) a rota of staff to man the stalls, so you needn't worry about that. I'll give it to you tomorrow. Don't forget the flights and hotel.

Luis That's all OK. My secretary _____ (already/book) the flights and she _____ (find) us a place to stay. It's a bit out of town but I think it'll be all right. It's called the Majestic Hotel. Do you know it?

Paola I don't, actually. I _____ (never/be) to Kuala Lumpur before. I'm looking forward to it.

B Now look at this list of jobs and tick the things that have been done so far.

> 1. *reserve stand*   4. *write copy for brochure of exhibitors*
> 2. *hire display equipment*   5. *find hotel accommodation*
> 3. *do mailshot for local customers*   6. *draw up staff rota*

C Now think of some preparations you are making at the moment. They might be preparations for

an exhibition   a visit   a presentation   negotiations   a conference or meeting a trip   a busy period   something else (what?)

Write a list, like the one above, of all the jobs involved. Include the things you have done so far and the things you still need to do.

Now write some sentences saying what you have and haven't done.

Example *I have taken care of the hotel bookings but I haven't sorted out the flights yet.*

_____

_____

_____

_____

_____

2 Attracting investment

Read this advertisement from a business magazine and put the verbs in brackets into the past simple or present perfect tense.

PORTUGAL
INVESTMENT JEWEL OF EUROPE

Portugal has a long and noble maritime tradition. Both Magellan and Columbus _____ (live) in Portugal, and their epic voyages _____ (help) to create Portugal's large empire which _____ (stretch) from Brazil to Macao.

Portugal's maritime heritage _____ (create) a great body of skilled craftsmen able to design and manufacture precision instruments. And although the age of great empires _____ (now/pass), these skills _____ (not/be/lost) and the labor pool is unusually gifted and well-educated.

When Portugal _____ (join) the EC at the beginning of 1986, the economy _____ (begin) to expand very fast. For the next five years, GNP _____ (grow) at an average rate of 4.6% and although it _____ (fall) a little recently, the country is still prospering. Since 1986, 120,000 jobs _____ (be create) every year, unemployment is only 4.1% and the level of strikes is lower than the EC average.

Since 1986, there _____ (be) a 33-fold increase in direct foreign investment. Many large multinationals including Ford/Volkswagen, PepsiCo, Samsung and Mitsubishi _____ (set up) operations in Portugal. So far, foreign investment _____ (come) chiefly from Europe but over the last few years we _____ (have) substantial Japanese investment and we are confident this will continue to grow.

The radical left wing government that _____ (come) to power briefly in 1974 _____ (nationalize) Portugal's banks and _____ (remove) the directors and senior managers of the Banco Espirito Santo e Commèrcial de Lisboa (BESCL). The group _____ (re-organise) themselves abroad and _____ (set up) an international banking network.

Today, Grupo Espirito Santo is stronger than ever; it _____ (recover) its former bank and _____ (now/become) the largest private financial entity in Portugal. BESCL is now more than ever Portugal's premier business institution.

Lisbon harbour

Amoreiras Centre, Lisbon

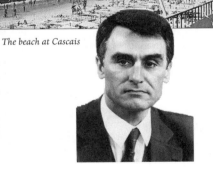

The beach at Cascais

Prime Minister Anibal Cavaco Silva

3 Word partnerships

Fill in the spaces in the chart using the ten verbs in the box. Each of the verbs is irregular, so be careful to use the correct form in the Simple Past and Past Participle columns.

fly	speak	give	ring	take	do	go	see	begin	write

	drive	a car	drove	a hard bargain	driven	carefully
1		well		up in price		bankrupt
2		a presentation		someone a rise		an opinion
3		the credit		early retirement		a chance
4		a report		a letter		in capital letters
5		a deal		your best		business with someone
6		eye to eye		someone at 10.30		the point
7		Club Class		a flag		by Concorde
8		work early		a meeting		to rain
9		to someone		five languages		up
10		someone up		back later		the bell

4 Phrasal verbs

Complete the sentences. Use the correct form of the phrasal verbs in the box.

| give up   hit back at   put off   pick up   pay in |
| tie up   take on   turn up   run over   Hold on |

1 I can't hear you very well because of the traffic. _____ a moment and I'll shut the window.

2 We were expecting them at seven but they didn't _____ until nearly ten.

3 We can't afford expensive holidays. All our money is _____ in the business.

4 I'll be driving past the airport at around ten tomorrow. Shall I _____ Mrs Schmidt for you?

5 I think we should _____ making a decision until we have all the relevant facts.

6 A lot of businesses need to _____ extra staff at this time of the year to cope with the rise in demand.

7 Is that clear or would you like me to _____ the main points again?

8 I'm just popping out to the bank to _____ some cheques.

9 At the AGM the Chairman _____ at his critics, saying they should be praising this year's results not criticizing last year's.

10 When he lost his job he had to _____ the company car.

5 A community action programme

Put the verbs in brackets into the infinitive or gerund form.

Example   We plan *to continue* (continue) our Community Action Programme this year.
We're going to carry on *making* (make) donations to community projects.

1   We will keep on _____ (provide) support for local education projects.

2   We have decided _____ (raise) money for the local secondary school.

3   At present the school cannot afford _____ (buy) all the computers it needs.

4   We hope _____ (set up) a number of different fund raising projects.

5   We hope that the students themselves will enjoy _____ (take) part in them.

6   In fact, the students have suggested _____ (publish) a local business directory.

7   We feel sure that other local businesses will not mind _____ (support) this venture.

8   And we have offered _____ (meet) all the costs of printing the directory.

9   We also want _____ (do) something to help unemployed school leavers.

10 We believe it is worth _____ (organize) a programme to give them experience of working in commerce and industry.

6 Money

Match the two halves of these quotations.

1   Money is...
2   Public money is...
3   Economics is...
4   A bank is...
5   Saving is...
6   A bargain is...
7   A fair price for oil is...
8   An accountant is...

a   a very fine thing. Especially when your parents have done it for you.
    Sir Winston Churchill (1874–1965), English statesman, writer, and prime minister

b   a place that will lend you money if you can prove that you don't need it.
    Bob Hope (b. 1904), English-born American comedian

c   a man hired to explain that you didn't make the money you did.
    (Anonymous)

d   something you have to find a use for once you have bought it.
    Benjamin Franklin (1706–1790), American statesman, scientist, and author

e   meaningless after a certain point. It ceases to be the goal. The game is what counts.
    Aristotle Onassis (1900–1975), Greek millionaire, quoted in Esquire, *1969*

f   whatever you can get plus ten per cent.
    Dr Ali Ahmed Attiga (b. 1931), Saudi Arabian delegate to OPEC, quoted in the Observer, *'Sayings of the Year', 29 December 1974*

g   like holy water. Everyone helps himself.
    Italian proverb

h   a subject that does not greatly respect one's wishes.
    Nikita Khrushchev (1894–1971), Russian statesman and premier of Soviet Union

10 Describing Trends

1 Graphs

A Read the three articles on the opposite page and match each one to the correct graph.

B Read the texts again and complete the graphs. Fill in

1 the figures in the right hand column.
2 the dates at the bottom.

C Look at these descriptions of the graphs. The first sentences contain adjectives and nouns. Complete the second ones using verbs and adverbs.

Example

There has been a dramatic rise in the Nikkei Index.
The Nikkei Index *has risen dramatically*.

1 There was a substantial fall in the Nikkei Index in 1992.
The Nikkei Index _____ in 1992.
2 There was a slight increase in the number of times Mrs Thatcher was mentioned in late 1991.
The number of times Mrs Thatcher was mentioned _____ in late 1991.
3 There was a steady growth in GDP in the Philippines from 1986 to 1988.
GDP in the Philippines _____ from 1986 to 1988.

D Here are some more sentences describing the graphs. This time fill in the blanks with adjectives and nouns.

Example

The Nikkei Index fell substantially in 1992.
There was *a substantial fall* in the Nikkei Index in 1992.

1 When Mrs Thatcher lost power, the number of times she was mentioned fell dramatically.
When Mrs Thatcher lost power, there was _____ in the number of times she was mentioned.
2 The Philippine growth rate decreased rapidly in 1990.
There was _____ in the Philippine growth rate in 1990.
3 The Nikkei Index rose sharply in September 1992.
There was _____ in the Nikkei Index in September 1992.

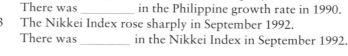

Margaret Thatcher with John Major

Election rally in the Philippines

The Stock Exchange, Tokyo

A The Thatcher index

As politicians go, few are as unforgettable as Margaret Thatcher. Ever since she was ousted as British Prime Minister in November 1990, her influence has lived on — often to the discomfort of her successor, John Major.

We asked a computer to count the number of times her name was mentioned in British newspapers between the last quarter of 1990 and the first quarter of 1993. Not surprisingly, her score dropped sharply when she lost power, falling from 5,634 in the last quarter of 1990 to 1,955 in the first quarter of 1991, but then it held up remarkably well at or above the 1,500 level until the middle of 1992.

Sadly for Thatcherites, it has since dropped again and her score of 1,275 in the first three months of 1993 was the lowest yet.

B PEOPLE POWER

People power was the slogan of the Philippine revolution in 1986, but sadly for Filipinos, the power that boosted GDP in the late 80s seems to be fading.

However, things are not as bad as they have been in the past. In 1984 and 1985, the Philippines experienced a major recession, with the economy shrinking at an annual rate of 8%. This was largely due to the austerity programme forced on President Marcos by international banks.

The revolution brought about a change in the country's fortunes and 1986 saw a growth rate of 3% which rose steadily to 6% in 1988. 1989 was also a good year, with a growth rate of just under 6%, but then the second recession began. By 1991, GDP had fallen to –0.5% and only managed to reach 0.5% in the following year.

C A NEW DAWN

This time it might be different. There have been many false dawns in the past 18 months on Japan's stock market. But the latest rally, which has seen the Nikkei average rise by over 20% from its low point this year of 16,500 in January, looks the most convincing so far.

This will be welcome news to investors who suffered heavy losses in 1992. At the beginning of 1992, the Nikkei stood at 23,000 and despite four very short-lived rallies in January, February, May and July, the index plunged to a low point of just under 14,000 at the end of August. September saw the index rocket to over 18,000, only to slump again to 16,000 in November. From then on, the market stabilized at around the 17,000 level and investors must be hoping that the latest rise to 20,000 can be sustained.

1

Sources: IMF; EIU

2

Sources: Datastream; Yamaichi Research Institute

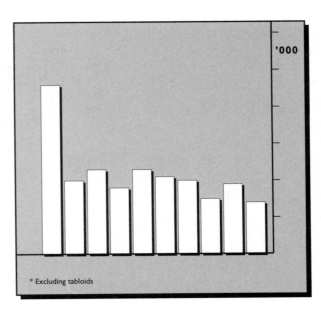

3

'000

* Excluding tabloids

2 Prepositions

Complete these sentences. Choose the correct prepostion.

1 The advantage _____ direct marketing is that it enables us to cut out the middle man.
   a on **b** from **c** for **d** of

2 What effect will this new EC directive have _____ the company?
   a about **b** over **c** on **d** to

3 BT shares dropped _____ 7p this afternoon and finished the day at 435p.
   a to **b** by **c** of **d** with

4 The government has spent less _____ defence since the cold war ended.
   a to **b** on **c** for **d** at

5 The phone lines are so busy that people are having to wait _____ an hour to get through.
   a up to **b** in on **c** out for **d** in at

3 News

Complete this puzzle and find the missing word.

1 We've made 50% of the staff redundant and _____ our wages bill. (6)

2 The latest figures suggest that the economic recovery is gaining _____. (8)

3 We've _____ enough money to finance another drilling operation in the North Sea. (6)

4 The manufacturing sector of the economy has been shrinking but the services sector has _____ . (8)

5 Our share prices have soared from 67p to 134p and our shareholders have _____ their money overnight. (7)

6 The political situation in Uzbekistan has _____ and some people are predicting civil war. (12)

7 The French franc has _____ as a result of the rise in interest rates. (12)

8 Sales of the new Nintendo game have really _____ off since the television advertising campaign. (5)

9 The world-wide _____ in car sales has forced manufacturers to cut production. (5)

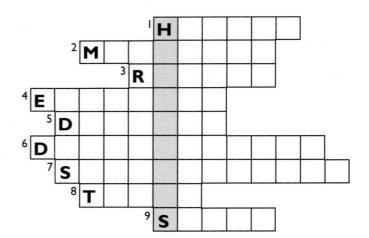

4 Probability

A Match the sentences that have similar meanings, for example, 1 — B — c.

1 You'll definitely get the job.
2 You're likely to get the job.
3 You might get the job.
4 You probably won't get the job.
5 You definitely won't get the job.

A There's no chance of you getting the job.
B You're bound to get the job.
C You could get the job.
D You'll probably get the job.
E You aren't likely to get the job.

a You may get the job.
b I'm sure you won't get the job.
c I'm sure you'll get the job.
d I expect you'll get the job.
e I doubt if you'll get the job.

B Rewrite these sentences in two different ways. Use the words in brackets.

Example

I might show your idea to the MD.
(may) *I may show your idea to the MD.*
(could) *I could show your idea to the MD.*

1 I'm sure the MD will like your idea...

(bound) _____

(definitely) _____

2 ... but he probably won't tell you that he does.

(not/likely) _____

(doubt) _____

3 He'll probably tell everyone that he thought of it himself...

(likely) _____

(expect) _____

4 ... and you definitely won't get the credit.

(sure) _____

(no chance) _____

5 Pronunciation

A Study the word in **bold** print in each of these sentences. Write whether it is a noun (thing) or verb (action). Mark which syllable is stressed.

The CBI reported a small **increase** in economic activity in the last quarter.
noun - <u>in</u> |crease
We expect economic activity to **increase** sharply in the next quarter.
verb - in |<u>crease</u>

1 When the Krone was devalued, Swedish **exports** became more competitive.

_____ — ex|ports

2 The negotiations are proving difficult. We're making very little **progress**.

_____ — pro|gress

3 The US is concerned that Japan **imports** so few consumer goods.

_____ — im|ports

4 I'd like you to **record** my objection to this proposal in the minutes of the meeting.

_____ — re|cord

5 There was a small **decrease** in the number of drunk driving offences this Christmas.

_____ — de|crease

6 Causes and results

Read these notes on a current trend in the computer software market.

Trend	Computer software market becomes more and more crowded
Cause	Large companies subcontracting development work
Results	Lower profit margins
	Some firms go out of business

Now read this paragraph, noticing how the ideas have been connected.

The computer software market is becoming more and more crowded. This is a result of large companies subcontracting development work. It will lead to lower profit margins and some firms are likely to go out of business.

Use the notes below to write similar paragraphs.

Trend	Car dealers report lower sales of new vehicles
Cause	A recent fall in demand
Results	A surplus of cars on the market
	Automobile manufacturers cut prices

Trend	Government revenues from taxation fall
Cause	The recession
Results	A rise in government borrowing
	Chancellor increases rates of taxation

Trend	Unemployment figures rise
Cause	Large scale redundancies in many industries
Results	Larger numbers of people claiming state benefits
	Public spending increases

11 Products and Services

1 Requirements

A Continue these comments. Use *must*, *mustn't*, or *needn't* and the words in brackets in your answers.

Example

It creates a bad impression if you leave the phone ringing like that.
(answer it straight away)
You must answer it straight away.

1 You can finish that report on Monday if you like. (finish it today)

_____

2 You were late again this morning. (get here on time in future)

_____

3 The phone is for business use only. (use it for personal calls)

_____

4 We haven't got any spare cash. (go over budget on this project)

_____

5 Our future depends on this contract. (make sure we get it)

_____

6 Attendance at this afternoon's meeting is optional. (come if you're busy)

_____

B Now continue these comments. Use the words in brackets again, but this time use *have got to*, *can't* and *don't have to* in your answers.

Example

We've got plenty of space in the new building. (He/share an office any more)
He doesn't have to share an office any more.

1 The car plant workers are very worried.
(They/accept a pay cut or face redundancies)

_____

2 Living in Saudi Arabia has its advantages. For example... (You/pay income tax)

_____

3 I'd like to buy it, but it costs too much. (I/afford it)

_____

4 We've had a lot of complaints. (We/improve our quality control procedures)

_____

5 We don't have enough staff to complete the job by Friday. (We/get it done in time)

_____

6 He has got a few weeks to think about their offer. (He/make a decision just yet)

_____

2 Instructions

A Here are some instructions for travellers, but they are muddled up. Match the two halves of the sentences.

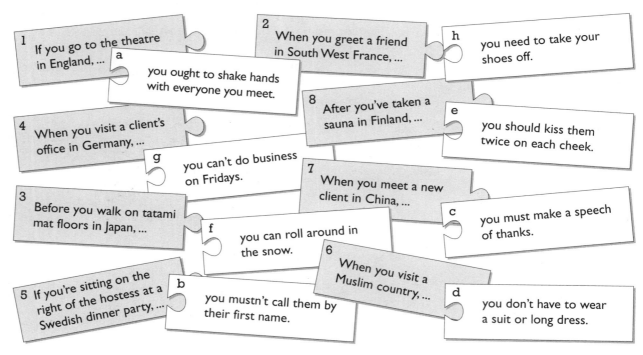

1 If you go to the theatre in England, ...

2 When you greet a friend in South West France, ...

a you ought to shake hands with everyone you meet.

h you need to take your shoes off.

4 When you visit a client's office in Germany, ...

8 After you've taken a sauna in Finland, ...

e you should kiss them twice on each cheek.

g you can't do business on Fridays.

3 Before you walk on tatami mat floors in Japan, ...

7 When you meet a new client in China, ...

c you must make a speech of thanks.

f you can roll around in the snow.

5 If you're sitting on the right of the hostess at a Swedish dinner party, ...

6 When you visit a Muslim country, ...

b you mustn't call them by their first name.

d you don't have to wear a suit or long dress.

B Now write some similar instructions for visitors to your country.

1 When you meet someone for the first time, _____

_____

2 If you go to the theatre _____

_____

3 When _____

_____

3 Technical description

The sentences below come from two different texts. One is a written text taken from a manual about a computer's spellcheck program. The other is someone telling their colleague how to use the same spellcheck program. Separate the two texts and put them in the correct order.

a However, if errors or new words are detected they are highlighted on the screen.
b Then you get a list of alternatives to choose from.
c When the spellcheck is finished, you go back to the document again and save it.
d If it does find a mistake though, it picks it out from the text.
e A list of alternative spellings is then displayed.
f The words in the document are compared with those in the computer's dictionary.
g Finally, the user is returned to the edited document, which may then be saved.
h The spellcheck program can be activated by clicking the mouse.
i You select the right one and the computer changes it for you.
j If no mistakes are found, the OK message is displayed on the screen.
k Then the computer has a look at what you've written.
l First of all, you use the mouse to click on to the spellcheck program.
m When the correct alternative is selected, the word is replaced automatically.
n If everything's OK, it says it hasn't found any mistakes.

Written instructions		Spoken instructions	
1	h	1	l
2	___	2	___
3	___	3	___
4	___	4	___
5	___	5	___
6	___	6	___
7	___	7	___

4 Formal writing

Rewrite these sentences in the passive.

Example

We make the engines for these cars at our plant in Munich.
The engines for these cars *are made at our plant in Munich*.

1 The recession has hit firms in the South East very badly.

Firms in the South East _____

2 We bring in most of our microchips from the States.

Most of our microchips _____

3 They have not fixed the date for the next AGM.

The date for the next AGM _____

4 They are printing the brochures this week.

The brochures _____

5 We received the last consignment six weeks ago.

The last consignment _____

6 They will make an announcement soon.

An announcement _____

7 We couldn't cancel the order because they had already sent it.

We couldn't cancel the order because it _____

8 If I had lost that much money on a project, they would have fired me.

If I had lost that much money on a project, I _____

9 We couldn't hire the building because they were refurbishing it.

We couldn't hire the building because it _____

10 They should do something about the terrible overcrowding on commuter trains.

Something _____

5 Following instructions

Follow these instructions and find the mystery country.

1 First you have to choose a number—any number you like between one and nine.
2 Now you multiply the number by nine.
3 If the number you have ended up with has only one digit, you do nothing. But if it has more than one digit, you add them together.
4 Now you have to match the number up to a letter of the alphabet. So A is one, B is two, and so on.
5 Now think of a European country that begins with that letter. Write it down.

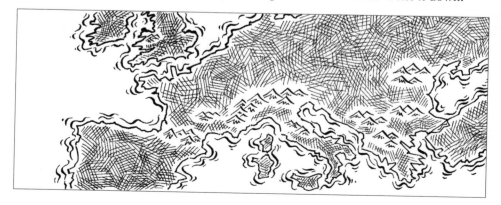

6 Word building

A Join the first half of a word from column A to the second half from column B and complete the sentences. Two of the words are hyphenated.

A	B
work	number
inter	chip
out	contract
micro	proof
ex	load
inflation	national
sub	wife

The interest rate on these saving certificates is linked to the retail price index so they are *inflation-proof*.

1 The _____ Monetary Fund is an agency of the United Nations, set up to encourage trade and economic development in poor countries.
2 Men still _____ women by about ten to one in top management positions.
3 We don't plan to lay all the pipelines ourselves. We're going to _____ some of the work to small companies.
4 Intel's new _____ , Pentium, enables PCs to process information even faster.
5 He's divorced now but he still has to pay his _____ maintenance payments.
6 I'm afraid I have no free time at the moment. I have a very heavy _____ .

B In English, several words are often formed from the same root. Make new words from the root words below to complete the sentences.

Example

produce
Henry Ford began the mass *production* of the automobile.
Looking out of the window is not a very *productive* way to spend your time.
Since the new equipment was installed, *productivity* has risen by 24%.

compete
1 We work on very small profit margins so our prices are very _____ .
2 Our recent technological breakthrough has given us a lead over our _____ .
3 The fall in sales revenues resulted from increased _____ from the Far East.

economy
4 Leading _____ are predicting that inflation will rise to over 2% by the end of the year.
5 Did you study _____ when you were at University?
6 The new Honda does nearly fifty miles to the gallon. It's a very _____ to run.

advertise
7 There's an _____ in the paper. It's for your job.
8 We can't print this article. Our _____ won't like it.
9 Which _____ agency do you work for?

direct
10 He resigned because he was unhappy about the _____ the company was going in.
11 I'd like you to meet Mrs Gardener—she's the new Sales _____ .
12 I don't know the telephone number. You'll have to look it up in the _____ .

C Now think of some more words formed from the same root words and write some more sentences of your own.

12 Comparing Options

1 Comparing products

You have done some research on three notebook computers and collated the information below. Your boss would like a short report summarising your findings and making recommendations about which model to buy.

1 Complete this paragraph about the Sharp notebook using the table and words from the box.

Supplier Sharp	
Model	NPC6340
Price	£1795
Battery life (hours)	2.2
Weight (kgs)	2.0
Height/width/depth (mm)	34-279-216
Documentation	Poor
Value for money	Poor
Ease of use	Poor

> the hardest   the least helpful   smaller   the most expensive
> shorter   the lightest   less   the cheapest   the lowest

In our survey the Sharp PC6340 came third. Although it was the (1)_____ of the three, it only cost about 15% (2)_____ than (3)_____ machine, so price alone was not a significant factor. The machine scored well in terms of size and at 34–279–216, it was substantially (4)_____ than the Apple. In addition, weighing only 2kg, it was (5) _____ of the three machines. However, we felt that these advantages were outweighed by the machine's disadvantages. One of the main problems was the battery, which had a much (6)_____ life than the other two models'. It was also (7)_____ machine to use; This was partly due to the documentation, which was (8)_____ of the three models. Overall, it was given (9)_____ rating in terms of its value for money.

2 Now complete this paragraph about the IBM notebook using the table and the words form the box.

Supplier IBM	
Model	N51SX
Price	£2060
Battery life (hours)	2.5
Weight (kgs)	2.8
Height/width/depth (mm)	53-297-210
Documentation	Excellent
Value for money	Average
Ease of use	Excellent

> more useful than   the longest   as clear   as easy   the lightest
> as heavy as   as good as   larger   the most expensive

Our second choice was the IBM N51SX. Along with the Apple, it had (1)_____ battery life—about three hours, so it would be (2)_____ the Sharp out of the office. Although it was not (3)_____ machine, it was not (4)_____ the Apple, and weighed only 2.8kg. It was (5)_____ than the Sharp but still small enough to be genuinely portable. It was (6)_____ to use as the Apple, and the documentation was just (7)_____. However, as it cost £2060, it was (8)_____ machine in the study and we felt that the value for money it offered was not quite (9)_____ the Apple.

3   Now write a similar paragraph explaining why the Apple PB 140 came out as the best machine in the survey.

Supplier Apple	
Model	PB140
Price	£1895
Battery life (hours)	2.5
Weight (kgs)	3.1
Height/width/depth (mm)	57-286-236
Documentation	Excellent
Value for money	Good
Ease of use	Excellent

In the survey the Apple came out on top for a number of reasons.

_____

_____

_____

_____

_____

_____

_____

_____

_____

_____

_____

_____

2 Connecting ideas

Join the two halves of these sentences. Use *if*, *when*, *unless*, *in case* or *until*.

1   The new offices won't be ready _____ December at the earliest.
2   Have a good flight and remember to give me a ring _____ you arrive.
3   You'd better make a copy of that invoice _____ it gets lost in the post.
4   The interview went very well and I'll definitely accept the job _____ they offer it to me.
5   Please don't disturb me _____ it's something urgent.
6   Before you leave to pick up Mr Friedmann, phone the airport and check his flight's arrival time _____ it's been delayed.
7   As you're going to stay here _____ I get back, I won't bother to lock up now.
8   I'd like to retire _____ I'm fifty.
9   We will be ready to sign the contract next week _____ there are any unforeseen delays.
10   We'll accept a cheque up to the value of £50 _____ you have a guarantee card.

3 Making plans

Complete this conversation. Put the verbs in brackets into the correct tense.

Anna Juan, I'd like to have a word with you about the visitors from Mitsubishi. If everything *goes* (go) according to plan, they *will be* (be) here on Thursday at 11.00. Can we just run through our plans for them?

Juan Yes. We (1)_____ (show) them the corporate video when they (2)_____ (arrive), then I (3)_____ (take) them round the compressor plant. After that we (4)_____ (have) lunch out somewhere and if that (5)_____ (go) well, we (6)_____ (talk) about the contract in the afternoon.

Anna That sounds fine but don't forget they may be feeling tired if they (7)_____ (have) a long journey. Are you planning to show them the IT system as well?

Juan Not unless they (8)_____ (ask).

Anna OK. There's one other question. If they (9)_____ (not speak) English very well, (10)_____ (they want) an interpreter?

Juan I think their English is good, actually, but it's a nice idea. If none of the other companies they have visited (11)_____ (give) them an interpreter, it (12)_____ (make) a good impression.

Anna OK. I'll set it up.

Juan Great. I hope everything goes well. It (13)_____ (be) really good if we (14)_____ (get) this contract.

Anna I know. And just think, if we (15)_____ (do), you (16)_____ (have to) start learning Japanese!

4 Opposites

A Add prefixes to the words in these lists to form words with the opposite meaning. Circle the words that have a different prefix from the others.

Example   *im*probable, *im*perfect, (*ir*responsible,) *im*mature

1   ____legal,   likely,   logical,   legible

2   ____reliable,   relevant,   regular,   rational

3   ____moral,   practical,   profitable,   possible

4   ____certain,   fair,   justified,   accurate

5   ____polite,   convenient,   formal,   dependent

6   ____organized,   honest,   similar,   efficient

B Use the words you have circled in exercise 1 to complete these sentences.

1   North Africa is the only_____ division in the group. It lost $15m last year.
2   It was rather _____ of him to ask us to leave like that.
3   Sandra is very busy. She's _____ to have time to see us this week.
4   It's a very_____ way of working. We're wasting both time and money. There must be a better way.
5   These statistics are hopelessly _____. I've found four mistakes already.
6   As cars get older they become more and more _____ .

5 Business expressions

Complete the sentences below with phrasal verbs. Choose a word from each column to put in the spaces.

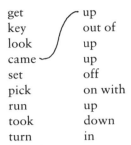

get	up
key	out of
look	up
came	up
set	off
pick	on with
run	up
took	down
turn	in

Example   Something urgent *came up* and he couldn't attend the meeting.

1 The business really _____ _____ when we launched our battery charger on the market. It was very sucessful.
2 We're going to _____ _____ _____ brochures soon. We'd better get some more printed.
3 Could you send a taxi round to _____ me _____ tomorrow morning at eight?
4 These files are confidential. You need to _____ _____ your password before you can access them.
5 Could you _____ _____ Elena Castagneto's number for me? It's in the phone book.
6 She borrowed the money she needed to _____ _____ the business from her father.
7 I wish he'd stop interfering and let me _____ _____ _____ the work.
8 Obviously we don't like to _____ _____ work but we don't have the tools we need to do the job properly.

SOMETHING URGENT CAME UP AND HE COULDN'T ATTEND THE MEETING

13   Meetings

1   A meeting

Three managers are holding a meeting. Put the sentences in the box into the correct spaces to complete the conversation.

a	Are we sure it'd save money?
b	Yes, I am.
c	That's true. We can't expect long-term commitment from people who have short-term contracts.
d	That's a good point. Any reaction to that Emilio?
e	It wouldn't be right. It would cause disputes.
f	It's a very good idea. It'd enable us to reduce our wage costs.

Elena   We need to decide whether we should subcontract the security work to independent operators. What do you think, Hanfried?

Hanfried   (1)_____

Emilio   Are you suggesting we should make the present security staff redundant then?

Hanfried   (2)_____

Elena   How do you feel about that, Emilio?

Emilio   (3)_____

Hanfried   Not in today's economic climate. We'd consult the unions and we'd try to get our present staff taken on by the subcontractors.

Elena   (4)_____

Hanfried   Yes – and it'd save time as well. We'd be able to delegate all the management tasks associated with security to the subcontractors. It'd mean we could concentrate on the core business.

Elena   (5)_____

Emilio   Yes, I don't like it. It'd be risky to have security staff who were not employed directly by us. You know what these security firms are like. People work for them for a couple of weeks and then disappear.

Elena   (6)_____

Emilio   Exactly. It'd be very short-sighted to subcontract this work.

2   Business expressions

A   Match the verbs on the left with the words on the right that they can go with.

1	accept	a	business, research, homework
2	do	b	mistakes, something clear, a suggestion
3	go	c	the truth, the difference, jokes
4	learn	d	a campaign, a business, up a bill
5	make	e	advice, someone a ring, in your notice
6	meet	f	a lesson, from your mistakes, English
7	run	g	the specifications, the boss, deadlines
8	tell	h	an invitation, responsibility, a bribe
9	give	i	on foot, bankrupt, first class

B Now complete these sentences, using a different expression from the list in each one.

Example   He's going to leave at the end of the month. He *gave in his notice* a few days ago.

1   May I_____ ? Why don't we hire a consultant?

2   I'm glad you liked our goods and everything went well. It's been a pleasure to _____with you.

3   I don't think we should take disciplinary action. I'm sure he has _____ and that he won't do anything so foolish again.

4   There was a tube and bus strike. All the taxis were taken so I had to _____ .

5   He's been dismissed because he _____ . He awarded a contract to Emporium and in return they gave him £300,000.

6   With these new ultraviolet scanners it is easy to _____ between genuine bank notes and forgeries.

7   The prototype doesn't _____ laid down by the ministry. We will have to redesign it.

8   She only stayed in the hotel for two days but she managed to _____ for over £1,000. The Accounts Manager was furious.

3 Review of prepositions

Choose the best word to complete the sentences.

1 If we leave now, we'll be there _____ plenty of time for the meeting.
   a at   **b** on   **c** within   **d** in

2 We work as a team, but we are all appraised _____ an individual basis.
   a in   **b** on   **c** with   **d** along

3 He must be retiring soon, because he's _____ his mid-sixties.
   a with   **b** in   **c** at   **d** on

4 Guests are presented with a welcome pack _____ arrival.
   a at   **b** by   **c** for   **d** on

5 I like Singapore Airlines, and I think their _____ -flight magazine is better than most.
   a in   **b** on   **c** by   **d** en

6 That's a very nice abstract painting, but are you sure it's the right way_____ ?
   a up   **b** down   **c** across   **d** over

7 Finance have asked me to remind you that you mustn't go _____ budget on this promotion.
   a past   **b** beyond   **c** over   **d** up

8 There's no need to shout — just speak _____ normal volume, and everyone will be able to hear you.
   a with   **b** at   **c** by   **d** for

9 It's not a direct flight — there are a couple of stops _____ route.
   a on   **b** en   **c** in   **d** by

10 What kind of canteen do you have _____ work?
   a in   **b** by   **c** at   **d** with

4 An interview

A Read this passage, then match the following interview questions with Bill Gates's replies.

Bill Gates, one of the richest men in America, had his first big break when his company, Microsoft, won the licence for the MS/DOS operating software for IBM personal computers. As a result, all PC manufacturers who wanted to mimic the IBM system had to use Microsoft's software. More recently, the company has had a huge success with their Windows operating system.

Questions

1 If you were to write your own job description at Microsoft, how would it read?
2 Do you go against the opinions of your colleagues? If you are completely alone, do you stick to your guns?
3 Would you say you are a good manager?
4 How do you feel if you have to fire someone? Is it easy? Do you have a strategy?
5 If you had been on the IBM board of directors, would you have put as much software power in the hands of Microsoft as they gave you?
6 Could you have matched your success in this business with equal success in another field, do you think?

Replies

a No, it's always very hard. I don't hire total bozos, so it's generally a question of the individual not meeting the demands of the job. I certainly don't have a method. I suppose if I have to describe one, I tell them verbally.
b Yes, I would. I make the right decisions. People are only interested in the quality of your decisions. If they are doing a good job, you should tell them so. Equally, if they are not, you should still tell them. Employees need to feel that you are sharing what they are trying to achieve and that you are constant in your decision making.
c No. And I certainly didn't wake up one morning and ask myself, 'What shall I do to be successful today?' I certainly never expected this success in terms of size or economics.
d You know, when we offered to sell part of the company to them, I would have taken up the offer if I had been in their shoes. I would have really tried to develop software efficiently, not just to license it. I would have learned more about the economics of software too.
e If it's a technical question or a strategy problem, then yes. However, if it's a business type decision, rarely is my conviction enough to go it alone. Usually I'd take the time to get people to explain their views more clearly.
f I'm the CEO so my responsibility is not precisely defined. When the company has to change, I'm the one who has to lead that change.

B Find words or phrases from the replies that have similar meanings to the following:

1 complete idiots
2 not in writing
3 the head of a company
4 exactly
5 strong belief
6 to act independently, disregarding the advice of others
7 in someone else's position
8 to give someone permission to produce something

C Match the two halves of these sentences about Bill Gates.

1 If he were to write his own job description ...
2 If he disagreed with his colleagues ...
3 If he had to fire someone ...
4 If he had been on the Board of IBM ...
5 If he hadn't gone into the software business ...

a ... it would say he has to lead change.
b ... he wouldn't have been so successful.
c ... he would tell them verbally.
d ... he would have bought shares in Microsoft.
e ... he would get them to explain their views more clearly.

5 Word check

How many verbs (actions) can you think of to fit in this space?

to _____ a meeting

Hidden in this word square are 16 possible answers. Can you find them all?

```
A S C A L L O F F S E
P T I N T E R R U P T
O A U X C H G M E O A
C R P L O N A G S S D
A T T E N D N S H T D
N Y O W T A I E O P R
C H A I R M Z Z L O E
E E R R O P E N D N S
L C A L L C L O S E S
```

6 Conditional

Complete these sentences about your career as in the example.

Example

If I had to write my own job description, it would say that I was in charge of the day-to-day running of the production department.

1 If I had to fire someone, ...
2 I wouldn't ignore the opinions of my colleagues unless ...
3 If I didn't meet my performance targets, ...
4 If I had a serious disagreement with my boss, ...
5 If I had the chance to work abroad, I ...
6 If I were asked what I liked most about what I do, I ...
7 I would be promoted faster if ...
8 If I thought of a good way of saving the company money, I ...
9 If I were in complete charge of the company, I ...
10 If I ever had the opportunity to change careers, I ....

14 Presentations

1 Introducing talks

A Here are the introductions to two different presentations. Separate the two presentations and put them in the correct order.

a   At the end I will suggest practical ways in which you as managers can motivate both yourselves and the people who work for you.

b   Good morning ladies and gentlemen, and welcome to our session on the dynamics of motivation.

c   Then I will give a short demonstration of our prototype and explain what we have already achieved.

d   Please feel free to raise questions at any time on technical or financial aspects of the project and I shall do my best to answer them.

e   To begin with, I shall outline the main goals of the project.

f   I would like to ask you to keep any questions you may have until the end, when I hope we will also have time to discuss your personal experiences and particular work situations.

g   Finally, I shall move on to the major commercial applications and potential returns on investment.

h   I will then turn to what we really mean by motivation, and look at the internal and external factors that play a part in creating it.

i   Good afternoon ladies and gentlemen. I would like to talk to you this afternoon about why we feel our interactive video project is worth investing in.

j   I shall start by looking at why motivation is so important and why the ability to motivate is a vital management skill.

Presentation 1	Presentation 2
b	i

B Read this introduction to a presentation. Choose the correct words or phrases in *italics*.

Good afternoon, ladies and gentlemen and welcome (1) *in/to/for* our seminar on corporate property management. I would like to (2) *begin/starting/commence* by (3) *drawing/telling/outlining* some of the main (4) *explanations/matters/issues* in corporate property management (5) *so that/for/in order* you will be able to judge whether your company is devoting sufficient time to this question.

I will then (6) *look/turn/change* to some of the legal and financial (7) *queries/aspects/pieces* of property management, and will (8) *tell/look/explain* how your companies may be affected by current and future legislation. I will (9) *illustrate/give examples/discuss* of the kinds of problems our clients have faced and explain what was done to solve them.

I will finish (10) *by/with/in* giving a brief résumé of the consultancy service that we offer, and I will explain what you (11) *need/shall/should* do if you would like to look into the matter further.

As we are rather (12) *hurried/pressed/short* for time, I would be grateful if you could (13) *rest/stay/save* any questions you may wish to (14) *rise/raise/arise* until the end, when I will (15) *do/make/have* my best to answer them.

2 Making recommendations

A Match the two halves of these sentences.

1 I found the hotel rather over-priced. I wouldn't recommend ...
2 The contract seems reasonable to me, but I suggest...
3 If you're looking for a good meal I can recommend ...
4 The strike won't last long. I would advise...
5 You need a very user-friendly computer, so I suggest...
6 I'd quite like to see a film and Jack suggested...
7 The bank manager was cautious about their plans and advised...
8 I have a month's leave and I'd like to study in England. Can you recommend...
9 Because of the risk of inflation, economists are advising...

a ...that new restaurant in Corn Street.
b ...staying there unless you had to.
c ...you get an Apple Macintosh.
d ...the government against an early interest rate cut.
e ...against trying to expand too fast.
f ...going to see *Basic Instinct*. Would you like to come along too?
g ...you get a lawyer to have a look at it.
h ...any good language schools?
i ...you not to give in to the union's demands.

B Continue these sentences in three different ways, using the words in brackets.

Example   The consultant felt that productivity could be improved. He...

(**recommend**)   *recommended setting the workers clear weekly targets.*
(**suggest**)   *suggested we should introduce some Japanese management techniques.*
(**advise**)   *advised us to invest in new technology.*

1   The stock market looks very risky at the moment. I...

(**recommend**)   _____

(**suggest**)   _____

(**advise**)   _____

2   I know the city well. If you are planning to be there for three weeks, I...

(**recommend**)   _____

(**suggest**)   _____

(**advise**)   _____

3   I went to a firm of career counsellors to see what I should do and they ...

(**recommend**)   _____

(**suggest**)   _____

(**advise**)   _____

4   The consultants have come up with a number of cost-cutting measures for our company. They have...

(**recommend**)   _____

(**suggest**)   _____

(**advise**)   _____

3 Reporting statistics

THE GREAT BRITISH BATH

British people spend a year of their lives in the bath according to a survey by Graham, a leading bathroom supplier. More than half read in the bath, a third drink coffee, almost a third sing, a quarter consume alcohol, around a seventh make phone calls and nearly a sixth use the time to clip their toe nails.

The Graham Bath Report published today indicates that three out of five people prefer baths to showers and that having a bath is an important form of relaxation for many people. 53% of the 2,500 people surveyed like to listen to music in the bath and over two thirds say they dream. Some tackle crosswords, and some practise yoga or meditation. One person in five says they watch television from their bath, four percent claim to have sexual intercourse and a few go to sleep.

On the more practical side, just under two thirds of the people wash their hair, a tenth use the bath to wash their dogs and others share their baths with pet rabbits and cats (particularly Persians). But for others, the bath is a place of recreation. 4% play with their children's toys.

A Read the article and complete this table of statistics. Fill in the missing percentages using figures from the box.

68% 62% 60% 52% 30% 25% 20% 14% 10%

What the nation does at bath time:

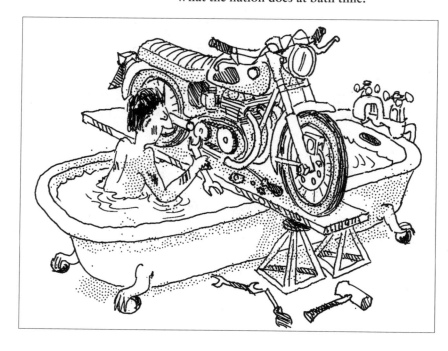

Read	
Drink coffee	31%
Sing	
Drink alcohol	
Talk on the phone	
Clip their toe-nails	16%
Prefer baths to showers	
Listen to music	53%
Dream	
Watch TV	
Have sex	4%
Wash hair	
Wash the dog	
Play with children's toys	4%

Example

B Re-phrase these statistics using fractions in your answer.

31% drink coffee in the bath.
Just under a third drink coffee in the bath.

1 25% drink alcohol

_____

2 53% listen to music.

_____

3 20% watch TV.

_____

4 60% prefer baths to showers.

_____

5 10% wash the dog.

_____

6 62% wash their hair.

_____

7 30% sing.

_____

4 Business expressions

Complete these sentences. Choose the best word to complete the sentences.

1 I think we should move _____ to the next item on the agenda.
   a through   **b** on   **c** in   **d** for
2 I hadn't invited him so I was very surprised when he turned _____ on my doorstep with a bottle of wine.
   a up   **b** on   **c** by   **d** in
3 I don't mind how you deal with the problem. It's _____ you.
   a down on   **b** in at   **c** up to   **d** over by
4 It didn't matter what we did. He kept _____ complaining.
   a from   **b** out   **c** in   **d** on
5 I haven't got the information here but if you ask Stephen he'll fill you _____.
   a up   **b** in   **c** through   **d** down
6 I'm surprised she didn't take _____ your offer. It was a good one.
   a from   **b** up   **c** over   **d** at

I THINK WE SHOULD MOVE ON TO THE NEXT ITEM ON THE AGENDA

5 Countable or uncountable?

English nouns can be divided into two groups, countable and uncountable nouns. With countable nouns we use words such as *a few* and *many*. With uncountable nouns we use words such as *a little* and *much*.

Examples

Can I make a few suggestions? (*Suggestion* is a countable noun.)
Can I give you a little advice? (*Advice* is an uncountable noun.)

A Are these nouns countable (C) or uncountable (U)?

help	money	machine
information	dollar	machinery
fact	baggage	equipment
knowledge	suitcase	tool
news	apple	work
progress	fruit	job
research	table	petrol
person	furniture	fuel

B Nouns that have more than one meaning can sometimes be countable in one meaning and uncountable in another.

Look at these sentences and decide if the underlined noun is countable or uncountable.

1 Is this the first <u>time</u> you have been to Africa?
2 We hope to save <u>time</u> by subcontracting some of the work.
3 We collect waste <u>paper</u> from the offices each day and send it for recycling.
4 I usually read the *Financial Times*. Which <u>paper</u> do you read?
5 She has a lot of <u>experience</u> in handling international negotiations.
6 I had a very interesting <u>experience</u> on my last trip to Mexico.
7 A decimal <u>currency</u> is much easier to work with.
8 These old coins are no longer accepted as valid <u>currency</u>.

C Now complete these sentences. Use *a few*, *a little*, *much* or *many*.

1 I've only been to Africa _____ times.
2 How _____ time do you hope to save?
3 We only collected _____ waste paper.
4 How _____ newspapers do you read each day?
5 Do you have _____ experience of international negotiations?
6 Did you have _____ interesting experiences on your trip to Chile?
7 Only _____ foreign currencies have fallen against the dollar today. Most have gone up.
8 Can we find a place where I can change some money? I only have _____ German currency left.

ANSWER KEY

1
JOBS AND RESPONSIBILITIES

1 Making contact
A Conversation 1, Mark and Karl:
j, c, f, m, a, d, i
Conversation 2, Josef and Sarah:
l, h, e, b, k, g, n

B Conversation 1 is more formal.

2 A first meeting
A 2 f 3 e 4 a 5 b 6 g 7 c

3 Prepositions
1 of 2 to 3 to 4 of 5 for
6 round 7 of 8 of 9 in 10 at
11 of 12 with

4 Word stress
B 1 <u>pro</u>/ducts
pro/<u>duc</u>/tion
2 res/pon/si/<u>bi</u>/lity
res/<u>pon</u>/si/ble
3 ex/per/<u>tise</u>
<u>ex</u>/pert
4 <u>or</u>/ga/nize
or/ga/ni/<u>za</u>/tion
5 <u>mo</u>/ti/vate
mo/ti/<u>va</u>/tion

5 Employment
```
1              r E c r u i t
2                M a d e
3                P e n s i o n
4        u n e m p L o y e d
5              n O t i c e
6  r e d u n d a n c Y
7              d i s M i s s
8              t a k E
9          r e s i g N
10  r e t i r e m e n T
```

6 Managing time
A She needs to discuss Italian accountancy principles in English with her counterparts in other countries.

B About an hour and a half.

2
TELEPHONING TO MAKE ARRANGEMENTS

1 Changing arrangements
A This is
me to
would prefer
Would you mind
No, not at all
would
that would be nice
if I booked
No
Would you

B 11.00 Meeting with Ms Watson.
12.00 Meeting with Mr Flavell.
1.00 Lunch at Wheeler's Seafood restaurant with S. Green.
4.00 Meeting with Mr Trigg.
8.15 Return to Paris.

C 1 He was seeing Ms Watson at 2.00, but now he's seeing her at 11.00.
2 Mr Boutin and Mr Flavell were having a meeting at 3.00, but now they're having a meeting at 12.00.
3 Mr Boutin and Mrs Green were going out for lunch at 12.00, but now they're having lunch at 1.00.
4 Mr Boutin was returning at 6.30, but now he's flying back at 8.15.

2 Polite questions
A 1 c 2 b 3 d 4 a

B 1 like me to send you our latest annual report?
2 mind if I had/took a day off next week?
3 like to fly Business Class?
4 mind waiting a few minutes?
5 like to visit our showroom?
6 like us to pay in advance?
7 mind if I paid by credit card?
8 mind parking over there?

3 Polite replies

A 1 Who's calling?
2 I'm sorry, could you repeat that?
3 Hold the line, please.
4 What can I do for you?
5 No, I'm afraid not.
6 I don't mind which.

4 Telephone language

busy, call, code, connect, dial, directory, engaged, exchange, extension, fax, hang up, hold on, line, modem, number, operator, phone, put through, receiver, ring, switchboard

5 Business expressions

1 pin down	2 come up
3 pencil in	4 is off
5 look forward	6 put out
7 bear with	8 draw on
9 tied up	10 put off

6 Emergency call

A a3 b6 c1 d8 e4 f2 g7 h5

B 1d 2e 3a 4g 5c 6f 7b

3
ORGANIZATIONS

I Present simple and continuous

A
1 is	2 has
3 plays	4 manufacture
5 meet	6 includes
7 is	8 owns
9 are	10 provide

B
1 is growing	2 is building
3 are designing	4 are expanding
5 is becoming	6 are reaching
7 are working	8 are dismantling
9 are removing	

C
1 manufacture	2 have
3 are working	4 are carrying
5 combines	6 are developing
7 are building	8 detect
9 warn	10 threaten

2 Number pronunciation

1a 2b 3a 4b 5b 6a 7a 8b
9b 10a

3 Number quiz

A 1 forty-nine 2 forty
3 nought point five 4 seventeen
5 two thousand and eight
6 thirty-two

B a2 b4 c5 d3 e1 f6

4 Business expressions

1 are on call
2 made redundant
3 give her a ring
4 rushed off our feet
5 losing his temper
6 get in touch
7 pick and choose
8 hand in my notice

5 Collecting information

1 Where are your headquarters?
2 Do you have overseas subsidiaries?
3 How many people do you employ?
4 What is your turnover?
5 How is business?
6 Is the real estate market doing well?
7 What are your current projects?

6 Storing words

B b Daniel Marchesin

C 1 shares
2 Stock
3 service
4 insurance
5 late
6 monthly
7 wages
8 Welfare
9 fluctuate
10 drop
11 get worse

D 1 b
2 a
3 a, c
4 a, b
5 a
6 a, c
7 a, b, c

4
PLANNING AHEAD

I Intentions

A 1 She's going to resign.
2 We're going to close it.
3 His figures are going to be updated.
4 This machine is going to be repaired.
5 I'm going to retire next year.
6 They're not going to accept our offer.

2 Future plans

1 'll ring
2 is happening
3 is Mrs Barberis coming, is giving
4 'll call
5 is retiring
6 'll pay
7 'm going
8 aren't we flying

3 Offers, requests, and suggestions

Suggested answers (others may be possible):
1 Shall I / Would you like me to leave my report with you?
2 I'll fax a copy of the article to you.
3 Will you excuse me? I'll just go and find my colleague.
4 Could you show a visitor around the factory this afternoon? I'm afraid I'm tied up.
5 I'll bring you a copy of my report straight away.

4 Prepositions

1 a 2 b 3 d 4 d 5 a 6 a

5 Green issues

1   r **E** c y c l e d
2   o z o **N** e
3 r a d i o a c t i **V** e
4   a c **I** d
5   f **R** i e n d l y
6   s **O** l a r
7   u **N** l e a d e d
8   w a r **M** i n g
9   n u c l **E** a r
10   c a r b o **N**
11   p o l l u **T** i o n

6 Letter-writing

1 Mr Jacobs   2 reference
3 conversation   4 enclosing
5 am afraid   6 wish
7 questions   8 hesitate
9 contact   10 look
11 hearing   12 Yours sincerely
13 Enc.   14 Thank you
15 pleased   16 would
17 if   18 could
19 convenient   20 appreciate
21 if   22 enclosed
23 forward   24 sincerely

5
GROWTH AND DEVELOPMENT

I A career history

1 until   2 at
3 later   4 from
5 to   6 before
7 after   8 when
9 in   10 soon
11 Since

2 A company history

1 How long did they produce light aircraft?
They produced light aircraft for six years.
2 How long has George Corby been working for Eagleair?
He's been working for Eagleair since 1987.
3 How long have they been manufacturing helicopters?
They've been manufacturing helicopters since 1988.
4 How long did they use engines imported from the US?
They used engines imported from the US for two years.
5 How long have they had a factory in Dorset?
They've had a factory in Dorset since 1990.
6 How long has George Corby been Vice-Chairman?
He's been Vice-Chairman since 1990.

7 How long have they been supplying helicopters to the Zimbabwe police?
They've been supplying helicopters to the Zimbabwe police since 1991.

3 Social conversations

1 I've been playing golf
2 We've known each other
3 I've been waiting
4 It's been ringing
5 I've had it
6 He's been talking to someone
7 I've been doing the manager's job

4 Word partnerships

1 lose, lost, lost
2 make, made, made
3 run, ran, run
4 take, took, taken
5 buy, bought, bought
6 go, went, gone
7 give, gave, given
8 read, read, read

5 Saying what happened

A 1 f, j, l
2 a, c, g
3 e, h, k
4 b, d, i

6 Business expressions

1 third world
2 joint venture
3 expense accounts
4 with reference to
5 press cuttings
6 glass ceiling
7 start from scratch
8 market share
9 working papers

6
PROBLEM SOLVING

I A meeting

should, feasible, do, How, negotiating, could, might, don't think, was, would be, had, start, about, don't, get, will be, That's, could, doesn't, will

2 Making suggestions

A 1 e 2 d 3 g 4 f 5 a 6 c 7 h 8 b

3 Pronunciation

2 guarantee 3 insurance 4 agenda
5 warranty 6 negotiation 7 colleague
8 advice 9 quantity 10 discount

4 Future possibilities

1 have / will read
2 will pick / haven't
3 had / would be
4 would be / was
5 rings / will pass
6 would hardly see / had to
7 will show / see
8 aren't / will sign
9 was / would be
10 was / would go

6 Clinching a deal

1 stayed up   2 look through,
3 ran out of   4 got round to,
5 slipped out   6 find out
7 point out   8 turned out
9 came up with

7
TELEPHONING TO EXCHANGE INFORMATION

I Asking questions

A 1 When did you dispatch it?
2 How many different shipments are there?
3 Does the first shipment contain the Rapidex plugs?
4 When will it arrive?
5 Have you received our payment for our last order?
6 Are you giving us a 10% discount?

B 2 when they want to leave
3 how long they are staying
4 if there are any British Airways flights around that time
5 they would mind flying with Singapore Airlines
6 if there are any seats available
7 when the tickets will arrive

2 Checking and correcting

hang, Ready?, Fire, was that, everything, there's, tell, run, Certainly, Is that, the lot

3 Explanations

1 where	2 who/that
3 when/that	4 whose
5 which/that	6 where
7 when/that	8 which/that
9 who/that	10 whose

4 Product descriptions

B Saracen – a plug-in burglar alarm. Its sensors can detect anyone entering the house.

Pentech 2000 – a superb pen. It comes with a matching biro and pencil.

Imatronic – a laser pointer. Its beam can point to charts over 30m away.

Mer – a revolutionary polish. It keeps cars in showroom condition.

Junghans – solar powered watches. They will last a lifetime and never need recharging.

Nightvisions – specially designed glasses. Their lenses cut out the glare of headlights.

C Saracen is a plug-in burglar alarm whose sensors can detect anyone entering the house.

Pentech 2000 is a superb pen which comes with a matching biro and pencil.

Imatronic is a laser pointer whose beam can point to charts over 30m away.

Mer is a revolutionary polish which keeps cars in showroom condition.

Junghans are solar-powered watches which will last a lifetime and never need recharging.

Nightvisions are specially designed glasses whose lenses cut out the glare of headlights.

5 Payments

1	Q u e r i e d
2	r e f U n d
3	c O n f i r m
4	p o s T d a t e
5	p l A c e
6	p u T
7	g I v e
8	b O u n c e d
9	i g N o r e

6 Business expressions

1 get a discount
2 kept on top of
3 fire away
4 make a note of
5 have any idea
6 ran like clockwork
7 had enough of
8 signed on the dotted line
9 frightened the life out of
10 want a word with

8
VISITORS

1 Meeting friends

7, 12, 1, 10, 5, 4, 9, 2, 11, 6, 13, 8, 3
1 2 3 4 5 6 7 8 9 10 11 12 13

2 Polite replies

1 e 2 c 3 j 4 g 5 a
6 h 7 i 8 f 9 b 10 d

3 Requests and offers

1 b 2 a 3 b 4 d 5 c
6 d 7 c 8 d 9 b 10 b

4 Experiences

1 Have you ever been
2 went
3 lived
4 was
5 Have you ever been
6 took
7 Did you have
8 enjoyed
9 did you stay
10 stayed
11 travelled
12 had
13 stayed
14 have ever stayed

5 Social quiz

1 b 2 d 3 d 4 a 5 c
6 c 7 b 8 a 9 b 10 c

6 Expressions

2 in having   3 for keeping,
4 for sorting   5 to going
6 of sending   7 without saying
8 on being   9 about moving
10 of buying

7 Food

vegetables: spinach, mushrooms, beanshoots, peas, parsnip, leek
fruits: melon, pear, blackcurrants, lemon, plum
herbs and spices: ginger, parsley, sage, pepper
fish: turbot, cod, salmon
shell fish: prawns, crab
meats: lamb, beef, pork, bacon
poultry: chicken, duck

8 Conversation topics

1 c 2 g 3 j 4 h 5 f
6 b 7 e 8 d 9 i 10 a

9
REPORTING ON PROGRESS

1 Preparations

A have reserved, 've told, Have you hired, haven't finalized, 've spoken, has already done, haven't written, 've drawn up, has already booked, has found, 've never been

B Jobs done: 1, 3, 5, 6

2 Attracting investment

1 lived
2 helped
3 stretched
4 has created
5 has now passed
6 have not been lost
7 joined
8 began
9 grew
10 has fallen
11 have been created
12 has been
13 have set up
14 has come
15 have had
16 came
17 nationalized
18 removed
19 re-organized
20 set up
21 has recovered
22 has now become

3 Word partnerships

1 go, went, gone
2 give, gave, given
3 take, took, taken
4 write, wrote, written
5 do, did, done
6 see, saw, seen
7 fly, flew, flown
8 begin, began, begun
9 speak, spoke, spoken
10 ring, rang, rung

4 Phrasal verbs

1 Hold on   2 turn up
3 tied up   4 pick up
5 put off   6 take on
7 run over   8 pay in
9 hit back at   10 give up

5 A community action programme

1 providing   2 to raise
3 to buy   4 to set up
5 taking part   6 publishing
7 supporting   8 to meet
9 to do   10 organizing

6 Money

1 e 2 g 3 h 4 b 5 a 6 d 7 f 8 c

10
DESCRIBING TRENDS

1 Graphs

A 1 Thatcher index: Graph 3
2 People power: Graph 1
3 A new dawn: Graph 2

B 1 *Graph 1*: 1 space = 2%
(minus 8 –12)
Graph 2: 1 space = 1,000 points
(12,000 – 23,000)
Graph 3: 1 space = 1,000 mentions
(0 – 6,000)
2 *Graph 1*: 1 space = 1 year
(1983-93)
Graph 2: 1 space = 1 month
(Jan. '92 – Apr. '93)
Graph 3: 1 space = 3 months
(Oct. '90 – Jan. '93)

C 1 fell substantially
2 increased slightly
3 grew steadily

D 1 a dramatic fall
2 a rapid decrease
3 a sharp rise

2 Prepositions

1 d 2 c 3 b 4 b 5 a

3 News

1   H a l v e d
2   m o m **E** n t u m
3   r **A** i s e d
4   e x p a n **D** e d
5   d o u b **L** e d
6   d e t e r **I** o r a t e d
7   s t r e **N** g t h e n e d
8   t a k **E** n
9   **S** l u m p

4 Probability

A You'll definitely get the job.
You're bound to get the job.
I'm sure you'll get the job.

You might get the job.
You could get the job.
You may get the job.

You probably won't get the job.
You aren't likely to get the job.
I doubt if you'll get the job.

You definitely won't get the job.
There's no chance of you getting the
job.
I'm sure you won't get the job.

B 1 The MD is bound to like your idea.
The MD will definitely like your
idea.
2 ... but he's not likely to tell you
that he does.
... but I doubt if he will tell you
that he does.
3 It's likely that he'll tell everyone
that he thought of it himself...
I expect he'll tell everyone that he
thought of it himself...
4 ... and I'm sure you won't get the
credit.
... and there's no chance you'll get
the credit.

5 Pronunciation

1 noun – <u>ex</u>/ports
2 noun – <u>pro</u>/gress
3 verb – im/<u>ports</u>
4 verb – re/<u>cord</u>
5 noun – <u>de</u>/crease

6 Causes and results

Car dealers are reporting lower sales
of new vehicles. This is a result of a
recent fall in demand. It will lead to
a surplus of cars on the market and
some automobile manufacturers are
likely to cut prices.

Government revenues from taxation
are falling. This is a result of the
recession. It will lead to a rise in
government borrowing and the
Chancellor is likely to increase rates
of taxation.

Unemployment figures are rising.
This is a result of large scale
redundancies in many industries. It
will lead to larger numbers of people
claiming state benefits and public
spending is likely to increase.

11
PRODUCTS AND SERVICES

1 Requirements

A
1 You needn't finish it today.
2 You must get here on time in future.
3 You mustn't use it for personal calls.
4 We mustn't go over budget on this project.
5 We must make sure we get it.
6 You needn't come if you've got other things to do.

B
1 They've got to accept a pay cut or face redundancies.
2 You don't have to pay income tax.
3 I can't afford it.
4 We've got to improve our quality control procedures.
5 We can't get it done in time.
6 He doesn't have to make a decision just yet.

2 Instructions

A 1 d 2 e 3 h 4 b 5 c 6 g 7 a 8 f

3 Technical description

Written instructions:
1 h 2 f 3 j 4 a 5 e 6 m 7 g

Spoken instructions:
1 l 2 k 3 n 4 d 5 b 6 i 7 c

4 Formal writing

1 have been hit very badly by the recession.
2 are brought in from the States.
3 has not been fixed.
4 are being printed this week.
5 was received six weeks ago.
6 will be made soon.
7 had already been sent.
8 would have been fired.
9 was being refurbished.
10 should be done about the terrible overcrowding on commuter trains.

5 Following instructions

Italy or Ireland

6 Word building

A
1 International   4 microchip
2 outnumber   5 ex-wife
3 subcontract   6 workload

B
1 competitive   7 advertisement
2 competitors   8 advertisers
3 competition   9 advertising
4 economists   10 direction
5 economics   11 Director
6 economical   12 directory

12
COMPARING OPTIONS

1 Comparing products

A
1 the cheapest
2 less
3 the most expensive
4 smaller
5 the lightest
6 shorter
7 the hardest
8 the least helpful
9 the lowest

B
1 the longest
2 more useful than
3 the lightest
4 as heavy as
5 larger
6 as easy
7 as clear
8 the most expensive
9 as good as

2 Connecting ideas

1 until   2 when
3 in case   4 if
5 unless   6 in case
7 until   8 when
9 unless   10 if

3 Making plans

1 will show   2 arrive
3 will take   4 will have
5 goes   6 will talk
7 have had   8 ask
9 don't speak   10 will they want
11 give   12 will make
13 will be   14 get
15 do   16 will have to

4 Opposites

A 1 illegal, *un*likely, illogical, illegible
2 *un*reliable, irrelevant, irregular, irrational
3 immoral, impractical, *un*profitable, impossible
4 uncertain, unfair, unjustified, *in*accurate
5 *im*polite, inconvenient, informal, independent
6 disorganized, dishonest, dissimilar, *in*efficient

B 1 unprofitable 2 impolite 3 unlikely 4 inefficient 5 inaccurate 6 unreliable

5 Business expressions

1 took off	2 run out of
3 pick up	4 key in
5 look up	6 set up
7 get on with	8 turn down

13 MEETINGS

1 A meeting

1 f 2 b 3 e 4 a 5 d 6 c

2 Business expressions

A 1 h 2 a 3 i 4 f 5 b 6 g 7 d 8 c 9 e

B 1 make a suggestion
2 do business
3 learned his lesson
4 go on foot
5 accepted a bribe
6 tell the difference
7 meet the specifications
8 run up a bill

3 Review of prepositions

1 d 2 b 3 b 4 d 5 a
6 a 7 c 8 b 9 b 10 c

4 An interview

A 1 f 2 e 3 b 4 a 5 d 6 c

B 1 total bozos (a)
2 verbally (a)
3 CEO (f)
4 precisely (f)
5 conviction (e)
6 to go it alone (e)
7 in their shoes (d)
8 to license (d)

C 1 a 2 e 3 c 4 d 5 b

5 Word check

address, arrange, attend, call, call off, cancel, chair, close, control, hold, interrupt, miss, open, organize, postpone, start

14 PRESENTATIONS

1 Introducing talks

A Presentation 1: b, j, h, a, f
Presentation 2: i, e, c, g, d

B 1 to
2 begin
3 outlining
4 issues,
5 so that
6 turn
7 aspects
8 explain,
9 give examples
10 by
11 should,
12 pressed
13 save
14 raise
15 do

2 Making recommendations

A 1 b 2 g 3 a 4 i 5 c 6 f 7 e 8 h 9 d

3 Reporting statistics

A Read: 52%
Sing: 30%
Drink alcohol: 25%
Talk on the phone: 14%
Prefer baths to showers: 60%
Dream: 68%
Watch TV: 20%
Wash hair: 62%
Wash the dog: 10%

B 1 A quarter drink alcohol.
2 More than half listen to music.
3 A fifth watch TV.
4 Three-fifths prefer baths to showers.
5 A tenth wash the dog.
6 Just under two-thirds wash their hair.
7 Almost a third sing.

4 Business expressions

1 b 2 a 3 c 4 d 5 b 6 b

5 Countable or uncountable?

A *countable*: apple, machine, dollar, fruit (can also be uncountable), job, fact, table, person, suitcase, tool

uncountable: help, news, money, work (can also be countable), information, progress, machinery, research, baggage, equipment, petrol, knowledge, furniture, fuel (can also be countable)

B 1 countable   2 uncountable,
3 uncountable   4 countable,
5 uncountable   6 countable,
7 countable   8 uncountable

C 1 a few   2 much
3 a little   4 many
5 much   6 many
7 a few   8 a little